W9-ABX-151

Organ Transplants

Look for these and other books in the Lucent
Overview series:

Organ Transplants

by Deanne Durrett

LUCENT
B·O·O·K·S

LUCENT Overview Series

Library of Congress Cataloging-in-Publication Data

Durrett, Deanne, 1940-
    Organ transplants / Deanne Durrett.
       p.   cm. — (Lucent overview series)
    Includes bibliographical references and index.
    Summary: Discusses organ transplants, including their history, the politics of
waiting for organs, ethical and economic considerations, solutions to the organ
shortage, and the future of organ transplantation.
    ISBN 1-56006-137-5 (acid-free paper)
    1. Transplantation of organs, tissue, etc.—Juvenile literature.
  [1. Transplantation of organs, tissues, etc.]   I. Title.
  II. Series.
  RD120.76.D87   1993
  617.9'5—dc20
                                              92-42990
                                                CIP
                                                      AC

© Copyright 1993 by Lucent Books, Inc.
P.O. Box 289011, San Diego, CA 92198-9011

Acknowledgments

The author wishes to thank all the individuals and organizations whose expertise and photographs contributed to this book:

United Network for Organ Sharing (UNOS), Richmond, Virginia; Regional Organ Procurement Agency of Southern California, Los Angeles, California; UCSD Medical Center, San Diego, California; Stanford Medical Center, Palo Alto, California; Organogenesis Inc., Cambridge, Massachusetts; Thermo Cardiosystems Inc., Woburn, Massachusetts; The National Bone Marrow Donor Program, Minneapolis, Minnesota; Dr. Norman Shumway's office; Senator John Seymour's office; Dr. Stuart Jamieson; Joyce Aaron; Craig Vollmer; Kathleen Woods; Malikha Abdolmutakabbir; and the Wednesday morning writer's group, especially Suzan Wilson and Becky Rutbrug.

Contents

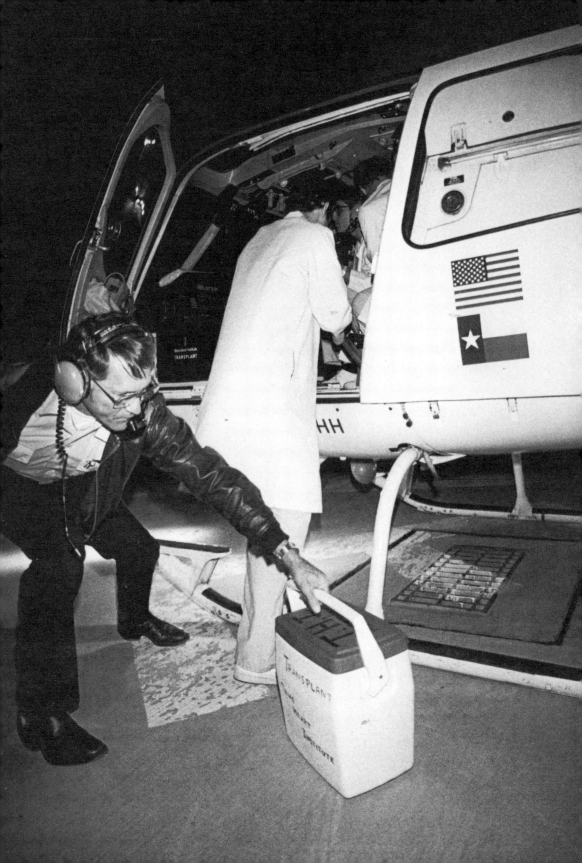

Introduction

THE TRANSPLANT PROCESS may begin in one minute, or two . . . perhaps an hour. . . . Then again, it may be days. The computer cursor blinks. The transplant team is on standby. Helicopter, ambulance, and Lear jet crews are on call, ready to spring into action. Across the nation terminally ill patients wait for organs. Day and night they stay near the phone or listen for a beeper.

Somewhere soon, doctors will fight feverishly to save a fatally injured accident victim, and lose. When hope is gone, even while the last spark of one life still lingers, preparations begin to save another. Phones ring. The computer search is triggered and transportation standby status is upgraded to alert. If brain death is declared in time . . . If the family donates . . . Then the transplant process will begin. Out of one senseless, untimely death comes hope for someone like Jacob.

"Thank you for your gift," says Joyce Aaron, of Mobile, Alabama, in memory of the stranger who donated a liver to her son, Jacob. "Jacob was born on May 14, 1984, but we didn't truly celebrate for him until May 23, 1990. That is when life began in the fullest for him."

Jacob was born with a rare genetic disorder, Alpha-1-Antitrypsin. The day he was born this

(Opposite page) A Lifeflight helicopter pilot reaches for the cooler containing a donated human heart, which he will fly to a waiting surgical transplant team in a nearby city.

9

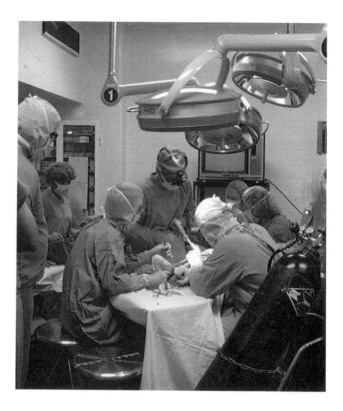

A highly trained surgical team transplants a lifesaving organ into the body of a recipient.

genetic disorder began to destroy his liver. Jacob went into liver failure in December 1989. He was five years old. His liver could no longer process protein properly and was sending pure ammonia to his brain. As his ammonia levels skyrocketed to five times normal, he suffered severe headaches and mood swings.

"One minute he was sweet and kind, the next he was screaming and fighting uncontrollably. Sometimes he wandered around in a daze, not knowing what he was doing," explains his mother. In January 1990, Jacob's doctors recommended a transplant. His parents took him to Ochsner Transplant Center in New Orleans, Louisiana. After physical examinations and psychological tests, Jacob was accepted as a transplant candidate. He was then eligible to be placed on the United Network for Organ Sharing

(UNOS) waiting list. Jacob's name was added to the list on February 1, 1990.

Three-and-a-half months later, one week after his sixth birthday, a liver became available for Jacob. The call came about 8:00 P.M. on May 22. Two-and-a-half hours later Jacob was on the road to New Orleans. Surgery began at 10:00 A.M. the next day and Jacob was in the recovery room eight hours later.

To prevent rejection, Jacob must take anti-rejection drugs every day for the rest of his life. Because these drugs suppress the immune system, Jacob must be very careful of infection. A common cold can mean a hospital stay. A trip to the dentist requires antibiotics before and after the visit.

Although Jacob is stronger and plays harder than ever before, he cannot play contact sports and must always be on the lookout for infection. He wears a Medic-Alert bracelet that identifies him as a transplant patient who must take medication to prevent rejection. Should Jacob be injured in an accident, the information on his bracelet could save his life.

In many ways, Jacob is the same as any healthy eight-year-old. He counts the days until Christmas and his next birthday. He dreams of the future and talks about what he will be when he grows up.

"Thank you is such a small word for this," says Jacob's mom. She mostly thinks of the donor whose gift changed Jacob's life. In fact, Jacob's transplant success was made possible by the donor as well as almost a hundred years of research and dozens of scientists from around the world who joined forces to perfect surgical techniques and attempt to unravel the mysteries of the immune system.

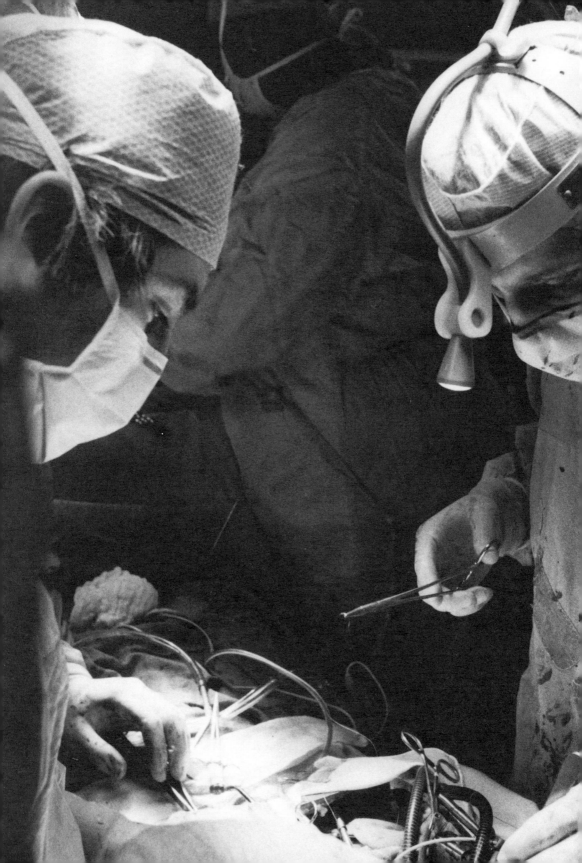

1

A Brief History of Organ Transplants

No SURGEON CONSIDERED organ transplantation possible until after the scientific advances of the twentieth century. Today's transplant successes are the result of more than eight decades (from the early 1900s into the 1980s) of dedicated surgeons' and scientists' refusing to accept defeat. Eight decades of scientists who asked why and surgeons who discovered how. And numerous tries that failed.

The first breakthrough

Many major medical obstacles had to be overcome before organ transplantation could be attempted. One of the first was the need to successfully join blood vessels. Since removing one organ and replacing it with another requires cutting and rejoining blood vessels, organ transplantation was considered impossible before this technique was perfected. Delicate and thin, vessel tissues are easily crushed. The needle and thread were too large and the vessels tore when doctors attempted to suture them. With no way to control bleeding, cut vessels bled excessively. In

(Opposite page) Amidst a tangle of tubes and clamps, a transplant surgeon carefully and methodically sutures a new heart into his patient.

13

In 1902, French physician Alexis Carrel developed a technique for successfully suturing blood vessels. Known as anastomosis, the technique is one of many that makes organ transplantation possible.

addition, when joining was attempted, blood clots formed when the body tried to repair the damaged vessel wall. Not only did these clots block blood flow but they sometimes broke away and traveled to the heart or brain, causing a heart attack or stroke. Before this century there were no drugs to prevent blood clots.

In 1902, French physician Alexis Carrel developed a technique for suturing blood vessels. Dr. Carrel used narrow bands of linen to control the bleeding and hold the vessel. He carefully cut the vessels without crushing them and shaped the ends to fit together smoothly. Carrel made three sutures (stitches) to hold the vessels in place, end to end. Then he used a very sharp, small, straight, round needle and silk thread coated with petroleum jelly. As the needle passed through the vessel the petroleum jelly sealed the puncture. Tiny, almost invisible sutures formed a watertight joint. This method is called "anastomosis," which means the vessels are joined mouth to mouth, or end to end.

Dr. Carrel developed the technique to provide a way to repair life-threatening knife wounds. He first used it on animals to rejoin the vessels of a thyroid gland. Later, along with his American collaborator, Dr. Charles Guthrie, Carrel began experimental transplants of tissue and organs in animals. With the new blood-vessel-suturing technique, transplants seemed possible and surgically successful, but the animals still died.

The natural reaction of the body

Dr. Carrel and other scientists reasoned that the animals were dying after surgery because their bodies rejected any transplanted organ as foreign tissue. Their reasoning was based on past research. Doctors had already successfully grafted skin from one part of a patient's own body to another. However, when doctors attempted this procedure from one person to another, the grafts always withered and fell away within a few days. From this experience Carrel and others reasoned that the body would not allow any foreign tissue to grow as a part of it. For transplants to succeed, doctors realized that they would have to focus on the whys of organ rejection and on how to combat that rejection.

Organ rejection happens as a part of the body's natural defense against foreign invaders. Certain white blood cells, called lymphocytes, search out and destroy foreign cells to protect the body from bacteria, viruses, and foreign objects. The body works to rid itself of a foreign organ much the same way it rids itself of a splinter in a finger. The white blood cells rush to the site. Soon the tissue surrounding the area reddens and a pocket of pus forms. The area swells and the tissue softens. In the case of a splinter, the foreign object is ejected along with the pus, and the wound heals. In the case of living tissue such as a vital organ (for example, heart, liver, lungs, or kidneys), white blood cells attack the tissue, killing the organ and the patient.

Organ rejection was further studied during World War II when bombers dropped incendiary bombs on major cities of Europe. Many civilians as well as military people suffered severe, extensive burns, covering most of the body. These victims did not have enough healthy skin of their own for grafting. The British government commissioned a surgical group to develop new methods of grafting skin in an effort to save some of these burn victims. The group included Peter Medawar, a young biologist. In the search for a way to graft skin from one person to another, Dr. Medawar observed skin grafts from one identical twin to the other. These grafts were almost always successful. However, grafts from one person to another still failed repeatedly. If tried a second time, the graft failed even more quickly. This led Medawar to think that rejection was linked to the immune system. He reasoned that the rapid failure of a second graft proved that the immune system remembered the previous graft attempt and therefore combated it even more quickly the next time.

Acquired immunological tolerance

Based on his observations, Medawar could have accepted the conclusion of a prominent physician of the time named Leo Loeb, who felt that organ transplantation was impossible. However, Medawar had read the writings of earlier scientists, including a Dane named Carl Jenses and an Englishman named Peter Gorer. These men had studied genetic makeup by transplanting cancer tumors in mice. In 1903, Carl Jenses had found that a transplanted cancer tumor would be accepted and continue to grow when the mice had similar genetic backgrounds. In 1916, Peter Gorer's work confirmed that the genetic makeup of mice determined whether they would reject or accept transplanted tumors. Medawar read Jenses' and Gorer's writings and compared their findings with his own observations of skin grafts between identical twins and between non-related individuals. In further research in 1953, Medawar injected mice embryos with cells from adult mice. When the embryos were born, Medawar found that he could successfully graft skin from the adult mice to the younger ones. This proved that the injected cells had altered the immune system of the younger mice. Medawar called this occurrence *acquired immunological tolerance.*

Through his work in genetics, British biologist Peter Medawar proved that a successful transplant required suppressing the immune system.

Medawar's work gave medicine the first understanding that suppressing the immune system was linked to genetics. This convinced many surgeons that human organ transplantation could succeed someday as more became known about genetics.

Additional evidence about genetics and transplantation came from experiments at the Brigham and Women's Hospital in Boston. In these experiments, dogs survived and remained healthy after an *autotransplant*—one of the dog's own kidneys was removed and transplanted to another part of its body. Because the kidney remained in the same body, there was no rejection. This added to the mounting evidence that the immune system was the cause of organ rejection. From these experiments and Dr. Medawar's findings, researchers theorized that kidney transplants could succeed if they were between identical twins. They assumed that since identical twins were genetically the same, there would be no rejection.

Kidney transplants

Kidneys were the first organs considered for human transplant operations. Since a normal person has two kidneys but needs only one, one identical twin could theoretically donate a kidney to the other. The problem was that very few identical twins could be found who needed a transplant. Since the incidence of identical twins is rare (about one in nine hundred births), scientists had little opportunity to test their theories.

Although a kidney transplant between people who were not identical twins had a very slim chance of success, in one case, a slim chance seemed better than none. In December 1952, a sixteen-year-old Parisian carpenter named Marius Renard ruptured a kidney in a fall from scaffolding. When the damaged right kidney was re-

Identical twins' genetic makeup is the same. This is why organ transplants between identical twins are successful.

moved, surgeons discovered he had no left kidney. As Marius lay dying, his mother begged Professor Jean Hamburger, a well-known kidney specialist, to take one of her kidneys and transplant it into her son.

After studying the findings of geneticists of the time, Dr. Hamburger reasoned that since relatives shared some genetic characteristics, their tissues were likely to be more compatible than those of non-relatives. On December 25, 1952, Hamburger performed the operation and Marius received one of his mother's kidneys. Marius lived three weeks, then his body rejected the kidney. Doctors were encouraged by the fact that Marius

In 1953, Dr. David Hume of Boston's Brigham and Women's Hospital transplanted a kidney into a man with a weakened immune system. The kidney functioned for six months before the patient died from an unrelated heart problem.

survived that long. Hamburger and others began to think that some tissue compatibility between relatives did exist.

Professor Hamburger continued researching organ transplants and teamed up with French immunologist Jean Dausset to search for more clues to the immunological mystery. Marius Renard had lived three weeks before rejecting his mother's kidney. Was it the fact that the two shared identical red-cell blood groups and subgroups (blood type) that delayed rejection? Would it be possible to find similar genetic markers in unrelated people?

Mounting evidence

Evidence was mounting that the immune system controlled the success of a transplant. But scientists did not yet have the knowledge to explain why. Dr. David Hume, one of the kidney transplant pioneers at Boston's Brigham and Women's Hospital, was encouraged by the results of Hamburger's transplant. Dr. Hume had a patient whose kidney failure had damaged his immune system. He reasoned that the damaged immune system might not react to a transplanted organ in the same way as a healthy immune system. Hume successfully performed a kidney transplant on the patient. In fact, the patient was discharged from the hospital. He lived about six months and then died of high blood pressure, not from organ rejection. This case offered more evidence that the immune system controlled the rejection process.

The first chance to prove the link between genetic similarities and the immune system came in 1954. Dr. David Miller was treating Richard Herrick, a twenty-four-year-old coastguardsman, for severe kidney disease. Fortunately, Richard had an identical twin, Ronald, who was willing to donate one of his kidneys to his brother. Dr. Miller referred Herrick to the surgical group at Boston's Brigham and Women's Hospital where kidney research had been done. Dr. Joseph E. Murray and Dr. John P. Merrill took every available precaution to assure success. Dr. Murray, trained in plastic surgery, first grafted skin from one brother to the other to determine that they were in fact identical. If the skin graft took, it would prove that their tissue was identical and therefore, they theorized, the transplanted kidney would not be rejected. They waited weeks for the skin graft to take. Meanwhile, Richard was kept alive on Dr. Merrill's artificial kidney (dialysis) machine. The machine filtered the wastes and toxins from Herrick's blood that his damaged kidneys were unable to remove.

When the skin graft finally took, the surgical team transplanted one of Ronald's kidneys into

Identical twin brothers Ronald (left) and Richard Herrick toast each other's health. In 1954, one of Ronald's kidneys was successfully transplanted into Richard's body. Because Richard lived for eight years with the transplanted kidney, medical historians deem it the first successful kidney transplant.

his brother on December 23, 1954. Richard Herrick lived eight years with his brother's kidney. When he succumbed to a heart attack his death was considered unrelated to the transplant. Most American medical historians consider this the first successful kidney transplant.

The eight-year survival of Richard Herrick proved organ transplants could be successful. The identical genetic makeup of the twins had prevented the immune system from rejecting the organ. Unfortunately, few people who needed transplants had identical twins. If organ transplantation were to become available to all who needed it, researchers realized, the immune system would have to be fooled or suppressed to allow transplants between unrelated donors and recipients.

While the search continued for the key to the immunological puzzle, surgeons such as Norman Shumway, Christiaan Barnard, and Thomas Starzl continued performing transplants and perfecting surgical techniques as they fought to save

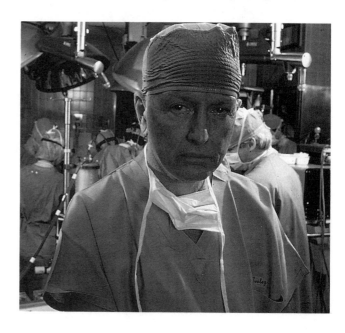

Prominent transplant surgeon Denton Cooley, like many of his colleagues, erroneously believed that surgical technique was the key to success in organ transplants. He stated, "The prescription for success in heart transplants is cut well, tie well, and get well."

the lives of their dying patients. At first it was thought successful surgery was all that was necessary for success in transplants. One prominent transplant surgeon, Denton Cooley, was quoted as saying, "The prescription for success in heart transplants is *cut well, tie well, and get well.*"

Cooley and others soon discovered the problems that so often ended the lives of their patients were not related to inadequate surgical technique but came from the patients' own natural defenses. Even so, doctors kept attempting transplants because patients had two options—the slim chance of an organ transplant or no chance at all. Death was certain without a transplant; with a transplant came hope. But inevitably, rejection would occur. Sometimes it took a few days or a few months, but it almost always occurred. However, although most of the early transplant recipients did not live long, their contribution to medical science and those who need transplants today was immense.

French scientist Jean Dausset isolated the biochemical factors of the body's immune system that trigger transplant rejection or acceptance.

Human leukocyte antigens

By 1958, Jean Dausset and Dr. Hamburger had isolated some genetic markers responsible for making each human different. These differences trigger the immune response when white blood cells come in contact with foreign cells, such as cells from a transplanted organ. Molecules on the surface of the foreign cells, called antigens, cause the white blood cells to produce antibodies. These antibodies attack the invading cells. This reaction can be viewed through a microscope when cells from two different genetic sources are mixed together. While studying these reactions, Dausset found a leukocyte (white blood cell) antigen that he thought might be responsible for the graft rejections.

These antigens in human tissue are called human leukocyte antigens (HLA). Researchers

An antibody (top) attacks an invading cell.

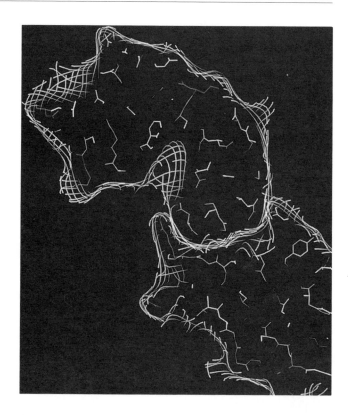

found that when an organ donor and recipient had similar HLA, the transplanted organ was far more likely to survive. The discovery of human leukocyte antigens was a major step in the development of the tissue-matching system that is used today to match organ donors with recipients.

Tissue matching, however, proved to be difficult. There are so many combinations of HLA that the average recipient has only a 1 in 100,000 chance of finding a complete match between non-relatives and a 1 in 4 chance between siblings. Even if a match is found, a living donor must be willing to undergo major surgery for the benefit of the recipient. (At that time the success rate for transplants from cadaver donors was so low they were seldom done.) For many patients there was little hope of finding a matching donor. If transplantation were to become more widely available, a way still had to be found to suppress the immune system or make the transplanted organ and the recipient more compatible.

Suppressing the immune system

Concentrating much of his effort on the immune response made surgeon Norman Shumway the most successful of the transplant pioneers. He was credited with performing the first successful heart transplant in the United States, in January 1968. During the next two years he performed twenty-six heart transplants. As a result of his efforts to control the immune system after surgery, Shumway's patients survived longer than any others at that time.

Norman Shumway's patients' survival rate (the number of those who lived) indicated transplants could be successful. Shumway had been using steroids to suppress the immune system in his research at Stanford University for some time, as had Dr. Thomas Starzl at the University of Colorado. Steroids, such as cortisone and prednisone, are chemical relatives of hormones made by the human adrenal gland.

Even with the use of steroids, though, Shumway's patients' survival rate was still too low. The majority of his patients still died. Many surgeons stopped doing transplants. They opted to wait until the immunologists and biologists could find a way to control the body's attack on the transplanted organ.

At first, the immunologists and biologists believed that a temporary solution was all that was necessary. They searched for a way to suppress the immune system just long enough for the organ to be accepted by the body. These scientists soon discovered, however, that T cells, the lymphocytes responsible for organ rejection, never give up. (*T* cells are produced by the *t*hymus.) As

Dr. Norman Shumway performed the first successful heart transplant in the United States in 1968. His success was due to his focus on the patient's immune response rather than on his surgical expertise.

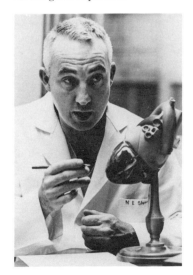

Transplant pioneer Norman Shumway (left) performs a heart transplant. Many transplant patients died due to infections that took advantage of their weakened immune systems.

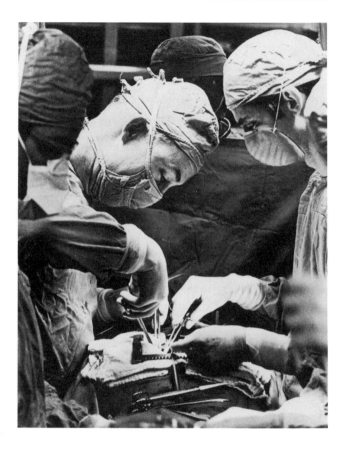

soon as the immune system recovers and begins producing T lymphocytes, the rejection process begins again.

Scientists also discovered that suppressing the immune system for a long period created a major new problem. With the immune system suppressed, transplant patients had no defense against bacteria and viruses. Under these circumstances the transplant wound frequently became infected and many patients died from bacterial and viral infections.

Double drug therapy

What scientists needed, then, was to find a drug that would suppress the immune system without rendering the patient completely defenseless against infection. Some researchers began testing the possibility of employing chemotherapy, using drugs that fight cancer to fight rejection in transplant patients. Dr. John Merrill at Harvard and Dr. Roy Calne in England were testing azathioprine, a drug used to kill multiplying cancer cells, for use in rejection control. In their research azathioprine also killed the lymphocytes that attacked transplanted organs.

Dr. Starzl added Dr. Calne's findings about azathioprine to his own studies of steroids and came up with a rejection therapy using both drugs. These drugs were prescribed in differing dosages to meet the individual needs of each patient. Azathioprine was taken daily as a safeguard

White blood cells known as T lymphocytes, or T cells, are produced in the thymus gland. They cause rejection of transplanted organs.

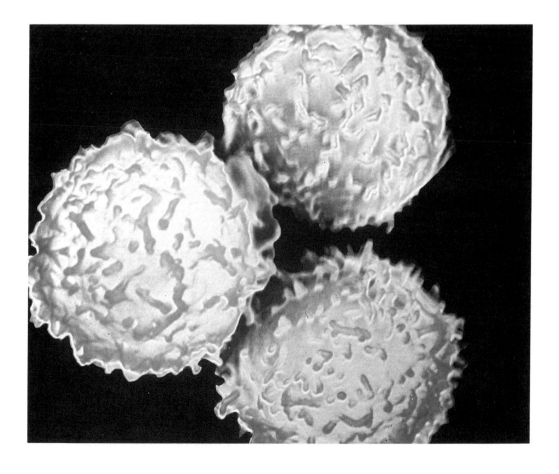

against rejecton. When rejection developed, large doses of steroids were used to reverse it. This drug combination soon became known as "double drug therapy."

To the scientist, double drug therapy was a significant advancement. More transplant patients were living longer. Yet, although these drugs were somewhat successful in controlling rejection, the side effects made life almost unbearable for the transplant survivor. The drugs made patients vulnerable to uncontrollable infections and lowered the red blood count, making them anemic. Many patients died from illnesses that were normally mild, such as the common cold or flu. The drugs also caused some patients to suffer

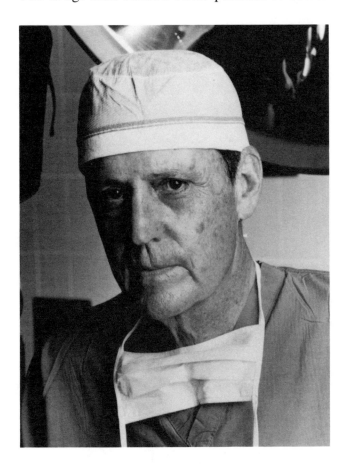

Transplant researcher Dr. Thomas Starzl developed the anti-rejection therapy known as double drug therapy, which uses a combination of steroids and anticancer drugs to prevent the rejection of transplanted organs.

from psychological side effects such as depression, mood swings, and memory lapses.

Dr. Starzl realized that even though double drug therapy made rejection controllable, the side effects kept it from being a desirable long-term therapy.

A great leap

An unexpected discovery in 1972 led to a revolution in anti-rejection drug therapy. A large drug company called Sandoz, Ltd., in Basel, Switzerland, was always on the lookout for microbes that might be used to produce new antibiotics. Such microbes had been found in soils, so Sandoz instructed their employees to bring soil samples back to the lab any time they went on a trip. One of their biologists, Jean-François Borel, was testing an unusual fungus found in a soil sample from northern Norway. In experiments with mice he noticed that one of the extracts from the fungus halted a number of immune responses without destroying the immune system. Later he injected the compound into a culture of lymphocytes (white blood cells produced in lymphoid tissue). As he watched through the microscope, the lymphocytes were immobilized but not killed. This compound showed properties never before seen in any immunosuppressive drug. Fascinated by his findings, Borel continued experimenting. By 1974 he had a refined substance he called cyclosporine.

Cyclosporine suppresses only one part of the immune system by paralyzing one type of T lymphocyte, called T helper cells. T helper cells detect the foreign tissue of the transplanted organ and signal the T killer cells to attack. Paralyzed by cyclosporine, the helper cells cannot produce the chemicals that signal the T killer cells to multiply and attack. Rejection is prevented as long as

Dr. Roy Calne, Britain's most renowned transplant surgeon, pioneered the use of the new immunosuppressant drug cyclosporine in organ transplants.

the helper cells are paralyzed.

In 1977, Sir Roy Calne, the most famous transplant surgeon in Britain, used cyclosporine to control rejection in dogs that had received transplants. Miraculously, organ rejection was suppressed, yet the dog's immune system was still able to fight infection. In his experiments survival time jumped from days to months.

Testing in humans followed in 1978. As with other immunosuppressive drugs at the time, doctors used the highest dosage possible. Although rejection was controlled, patients suffered kidney damage and developed lymphoma (cancer involving the lymph glands). Discouraged, researchers considered abandoning the drug.

Fortunately, testing continued. In other experiments, cyclosporine was used in combination with steroids. Researchers soon found that it was the dosage, not the drug, that was causing the problems. They discovered that the dosage of cyclosporine had to be adjusted for each patient. Large doses were given at first, and then the dosage was gradually reduced until the patient was taking the exact amount needed to prevent organ rejection and still allow the unaffected lymphocytes to fight infection.

One major drawback to cyclosporine was that it could not be taken orally. It did not enter the bloodstream from the digestive system, so it had to be injected. This was difficult for transplant patients who had to take the drug daily—for the rest of their lives. Researchers involved in the testing of cyclosporine searched for a liquid that would make oral dosage possible. Doctors eventually found that olive oil helped cyclosporine make its way to the bloodstream.

In 1980, eighteen-year-old Dan Krainert was one of the first to participate in the human experiments with cyclosporine at Stanford University. According to *A Gift of Life* by S. Rickly Christian, Krainert's nurse coaxed him to take his first dose of the foul-tasting cyclosporine by telling him he was "the first person in the world to use it." Krainert, a heart transplant patient, is still doing well more than twelve years after the transplant.

A lifetime commitment

In 1981, a refined version of cyclosporine, nicknamed the "Magic Bullet," was developed. In 1983, the Food and Drug Administration (FDA) approved cyclosporine for use in human transplant patients in the United States. Transplant survival rates climbed.

Research continues, both to find new drugs and

These athletes are all organ transplant recipients. They are competing in the 1992 Transplant Games in Los Angeles. The Olympics-style event demonstrates that, today, transplant recipients can not only survive, but also can lead physically active lives.

to refine the current ones. As a result of these efforts, today's transplant specialist has an arsenal of immunosuppressive drugs at his command. Cyclosporine, alone or combined with a variety of other drugs, is able to control most rejection. Since the immune system is merely immobilized, not destroyed, the white blood cells will begin to recover as soon as the anti-rejection (immunosuppressive) drugs are out of the system. Therefore a transplant patient must take the medication faithfully for the rest of his or her life. Failure to take the medication, even just once or twice, can mean organ rejection and possible death.

Transplant patients are carefully monitored for rejection, and some undergo routine biopsies of the transplanted organ. Biopsies are especially helpful in detecting rejection of transplanted hearts. To do a heart biopsy, a small catheter is threaded through a vein in the neck and guided to the heart. A sliver of tissue about the size of a grain of rice is removed with a tweezerlike instrument. This tissue is then examined under the microscope for the presence of T cells. If rejection is detected, adjusting the drug therapy usually reverses it. Biopsies are required because rejection in patients using cyclosporine progresses very slowly and is difficult to diagnose in the early stages.

Side effects, such as vulnerability to infection, excessive hair growth, tremors, gum overgrowth, kidney damage, and high blood pressure, although milder than those of the other drugs, are still a problem, so the search for better immunosuppressive drugs goes on. Yet scientists have come a long way since 1900. Today, hundreds of people are living with a transplanted organ when a century ago they would have faced certain death.

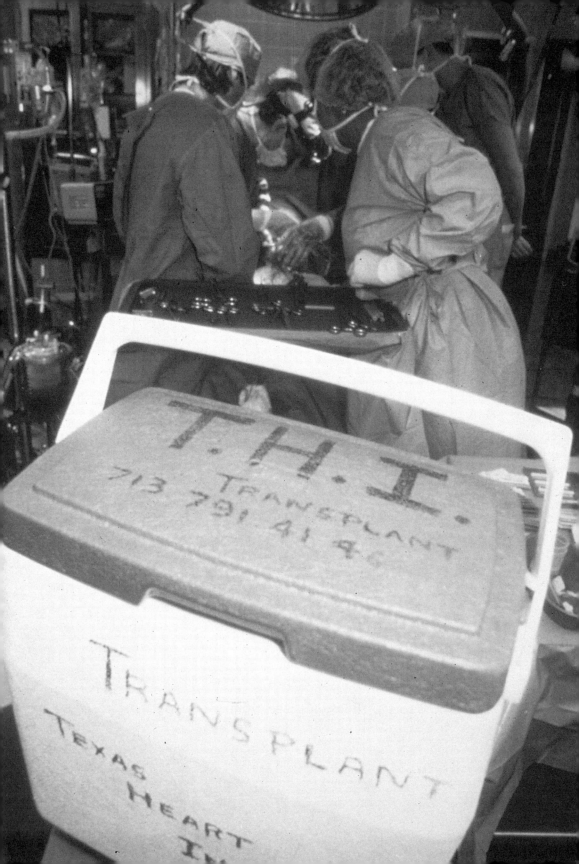

2

Organ Transplants: The Who, What, Why, and How

WHEN A VITAL ORGAN, such as a heart or liver, fails to function and cannot be treated in any other way, the patient's only chance to live is to undergo an organ transplant. According to the United Network for Organ Sharing (UNOS), 16,003 organ transplants were performed in the United States in 1991:

9,943 kidney transplants
2,946 liver transplants
2,127 heart transplants
535 pancreas transplants
400 lung transplants
52 heart-lung transplants

While the demand for organs grows by the thousands, the number of donors per year has only increased by a few hundred, from 4,000 in 1988 to less than 4,350 in 1990. As a result, organ recipients must often wait a long time for a transplant. For example, the average wait for a

(Opposite page) A common ice chest is used to transport organs from the donor to the recipient.

kidney is more than a year, while the average wait for a heart-lung transplant is two years. For about 30 percent of the patients on a waiting list for a vital organ, time runs out. In 1991, more than 2,500 adults and children died while waiting for organs.

Who needs a transplant?

While organ recipients are of different races, genders, and ages, the number of each type of transplant varies according to these factors. The reason for this is that certain diseases tend to strike certain groups of people more often. For instance, children are more likely than adults to be victims of leukemia; therefore, more children need bone-marrow transplants than adults. Men have a higher percentage of heart disease than women, so they need heart transplants more often than women. Kidney disease strikes a higher percentage of blacks than any other race, so blacks need more kidney transplants than anyone else.

Patients Who Received Transplants and Patients Who Died Waiting for Transplants

	Patients on List	New Patients on List	Transplant Received	Patients Who Died Waiting
Oct-Dec 1987	13,168	4,695	2,053	291
Jan-Mar 1988	14,332	4,411	2,172	376
Apr-Jun 1988	14,766	4,153	2,512	393
Jul-Sep 1988	15,395	4,484	2,654	433
Oct-Dec 1988	16,035	4,368	2,644	414
Jan-Mar 1989	16,966	4,764	2,609	516
Apr-Jun 1989	17,705	4,665	2,705	456
Jul-Sep 1989	18,511	4,728	2,732	396
Oct-Dec 1989	19,173	4,789	2,830	510
Jan-Mar 1990	20,177	5,169	2,875	565

The United Network for Organ Sharing (UNOS) in Richmond, Virginia, serves as a vital link between donor organs and patients awaiting transplants.

All patients seeking solid organs (such as a heart, lung, liver, kidney, or pancreas) are registered with UNOS, located in Richmond, Virginia. UNOS is a private organization under contract with the U.S. Department of Health and Human Services. Twenty-four hours a day, the network connects 266 transplant centers (hospitals certified to do organ transplants) with 51 independent regional organ-procurement organizations. When an organ becomes available, a recipient is sought from the UNOS list in the local area of the donor. If no suitable recipient is found, the area is extended to include the region. If still no recipient is found, the search is expanded nationally.

Only patients listed with UNOS are considered in the search for a recipient for a donor organ. In order to be listed, a patient seeking a transplant must be referred to one of the transplant centers by his or her personal doctor. The transplant center screens each patient, and the decision to "list" the patient is up to the transplant center doctor. If a transplant is determined to be the patient's only option, other points are then considered, including an estimate of the patient's chances of surviving the surgery. The patient's general health is evaluated, along with the condition of other vital organs. The transplant doctor must consider whether a transplant for this patient would be the best use of a scarce resource—a donated organ.

The patient is also psychologically evaluated to determine whether he or she has a strong-enough will to live. The doctor tries to judge whether the patient will follow doctor's orders, stay on the recommended diet, and take the daily anti-rejection drugs without fail. If the patient is a child, the parents are evaluated to determine whether they are responsible and reliable, and capable of taking on the child's care after surgery.

Economic considerations are also taken into account. If Medicare or private insurance will not cover the transplant, the patient will have to post as much as $100,000 before being listed. Those

Surgeons prepare a donated kidney for transplantation.

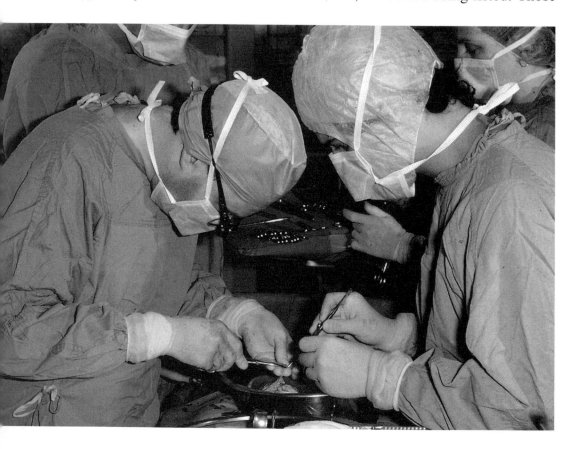

without insurance who have the money will be listed immediately. Those who have neither insurance nor money will not be listed until they can raise the money. In addition to the costs of the surgery, the anti-rejection drugs the organ recipient must take for the rest of his or her life are expensive, generally costing $3,000 to $10,000 a year; these costs are also considered.

Life on the list

No one is number one on the list, although length of time listed is considered when other factors are equal. Organs are unique and usually a custom fit. The person with the most urgent need and the closest HLA (human leukocyte antigen) match will receive the kidney or pancreas. Hearts, livers, and lungs are not HLA matched—for these organs, body size, blood type, and distance from the donor hospital are the deciding factors. For example, when a heart becomes available there may be only one 180-pound person with blood type B on the heart list who is close enough to the donor hospital to receive the transplant within the four-to-six-hour limit. Occasionally, there are two recipients who are the same size, have a compatible blood type, and are equally close to the hospital. In this case, the transplant doctor makes the decision based on factors he or she considers most important to make the best use of the organs.

If it were possible, all transplanted organs would be HLA matched. Since the immune system identifies foreign HLA codes and attacks and destroys cells that are not a match, an HLA match would ensure the body's acceptance of the organ. This would eliminate the need for anti-rejection drugs and make life much better for the transplant recipients. Many factors prevent HLA matching. For one, a perfect HLA match is rare. Countless combinations of the HLA codes exist. The chance

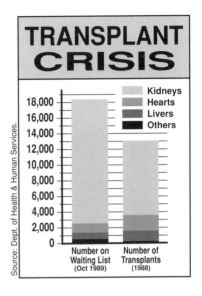

that two unrelated people will have the same HLA combination may be as good as one in twenty thousand or as unlikely as one in a million, depending on the ethnic background. Between siblings, there is a one in four chance of an HLA match.

Another factor that interferes with finding a perfect HLA match is that donor organs must be transplanted within a certain time. Once the organs are removed, ischemic time, or the time the organs can be kept out of the body without blood circulating through them, is limited. Hearts and lungs must be transplanted within four to six hours, and the pancreas and liver within twenty-four hours, while kidneys are good up to seventy-two hours. In addition to these time limits, patients who need a heart, lung, or liver usually do not live long enough for an organ of both the right size and the right tissue type to become available.

Those who wait

For every person who waits for an organ, time is critical. Whether the wait is for matching bone marrow or a solid organ such as a heart or liver, a patient can die before a donor organ is found. The wait varies depending on the demand for and scarcity of the organ as well as the degree of HLA match required. Kidneys, for example, are in tremendous demand and must have at least a partial HLA match. As a result, the average wait for a kidney is more than a year.

The outlook is even worse for those who wait for bone marrow. Because a successful marrow transplant requires a perfect genetic match, only 30 percent of the patients who request a search of the half-million volunteer donors listed with the National Marrow Donor Program will find a match. Fifteen-year-old Tailleur McGreevy, for

The National Marrow Donor Program uses advertisements like this one to help locate possible donors.

You Could Make the Difference for Askia

Askia needs a bone marrow transplant to cure a fatal blood disease. He is searching for a matched donor who can offer him the Chance of a Lifetime.

National Marrow Donor Program 1–800–654–1247

example, died before she found a marrow donor. When no donor was found on the national list, more than a thousand people volunteered to be tested as possible donors, but still a match could not be found.

When a patient is listed with UNOS for a solid organ, no one knows how long the wait will be. During this time family members are sometimes separated because the patient must stay within an hour of the transplant center. Some patients camp near the hospital in motor homes or rent small apartments. Others stay at places like a Ronald McDonald House. Often one member of the family will stay with the patient while the rest of the family tries to keep some normality in life at home.

Since the good news may come at any time, all patients wear beepers whenever they are away from a phone. Thus, often away from home and separated from family and friends, the patient waits for "the call."

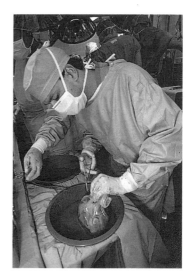

A member of a heart transplant team removes a donated heart from the plastic bag in which it was transported.

The transplant process

When a donor organ becomes available, "the call" is made as soon as the recipient has been determined. About the time the transplant team leaves for the donor hospital, the recipient is instructed to report to the transplant center. From the moment the transplant process begins, constant communication between the transplant team and the transplant center is absolutely necessary. Every move is coordinated with precision because every minute the organ is out of the body, cells are dying.

As soon as an organ such as the heart is removed and packaged for transport, the transplant team runs from the operating room to a waiting helicopter or ambulance with the organ packed in ice in a small ice chest. If it is far to the transplant

Marrow Collection Process

Chances are low that a National Marrow Donor Program volunteer will be a match for a patient with a fatal blood disease. If a match occurs and the volunteer agrees to be a donor, this is the procedure:

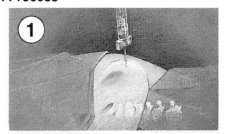

1. A Living Gift of Life

Marrow is taken from the back of the pelvic bone (iliac crest). Less than 10% of the donor's marrow is collected and the marrow replenishes itself within a few weeks. A donor's marrow contains stem cells which, if they grow in the patient, will begin producing healthy blood cells.

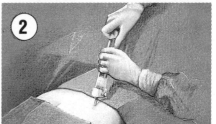

2. A Surgical Procedure

Under anesthesia, marrow is taken, or aspirated, from the donor using a needle and syringe.

3. Repeated Aspirations Are Pooled

If the recipient is a baby, a "coffee cup" of marrow is needed; a large adult patient may need as much as a "coffee pot." The bone cavities which contain marrow are honeycomb shaped and therefore several needle aspirations may be needed. The small incisions in the skin are treated with one large or several small bandages. Some donors remember the most painful part of the whole process to be when the bandage is pulled off the skin!

4. Patient Receives the Gift of a Stranger

The donor's marrow is flown to the patient the same day and given like a blood transfusion. The stem cells are "smart" enough to travel to the inside of the patient's bones.

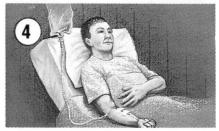

center, the team will be rushed to a waiting Lear jet. Once the jet touches down at the designated airport, a waiting helicopter or ambulance will rush the team to the transplant center.

The patient is prepped and anesthetized while the heart is en route. Although the incision is made in the recipient as the transplant team nears the center, the recipient's heart is not removed until the donor heart is actually in the operating room. The same surgeon who removed the heart from the donor will transplant it into the recipient.

A specific procedure is followed for procuring the donor organs. Each organ is removed in order by a different surgical team, usually the same team that will transplant the organ. All vital organs are packaged for transport in about the same manner. For example, after the heart is removed, it is rinsed in an ice-cold, sterile solution, then slipped into a plastic bag filled with more of the cold solution. This bag is closed with an ordinary supermarket twist tie and slipped into a second bag. The second bag is closed and then sealed in a plastic container. The plastic container with its lifesaving contents is then packed in ice in an ordinary insulated picnic chest and rushed to the transplant center where the recipient is waiting.

Reaching the recipient

If the transplant center cannot reach the recipient on the first try, it will sometimes go to extraordinary measures. This was the case when the donor heart for Dan Krainert became available in 1980. Krainert had moved to Palo Alto, California, to be near the transplant center at Stanford University. That December, he decided to go back to his Napa Valley home for the holidays. While he was on the road between Palo Alto and Napa Valley, his call came. When he was not found at the Palo Alto apartment, the message was broadcast by all area radio stations. Unfortunately the Krainerts were not listening to their car radio. The California Highway Patrol was alerted but failed to intercept them. The news was waiting when the Krainerts reached the family home in Napa Valley at 3:25 P.M. Dan had to be back at the hospital by 4:30 or the heart would go to another patient. Fortunately, his aunt and the California Highway Patrol had already arranged for a

A member of a transplant team lifts a donated kidney out of its beaker of ice.

In order for a potential donor's organs to be used, a donor card must be signed.

charter plane to fly him to Palo Alto. An ambulance waiting at the Palo Alto airport whisked him to the hospital, where he arrived to claim his heart with four minutes to spare.

Dan Krainert was lucky. In most cases the waiting patient is getting sicker, weaker, and closer to death with every day that passes. According to commentary in the *Journal of the American Medical Association*, in the first three months of 1990, 565 people died out of the 20,177 patients waiting on the UNOS list.

Too few organs

Why are more organs not available? Many factors complicate the issue. Organ donation is strictly voluntary, and as a result many organs are not donated because the potential donor has not filled out a donor card or made his or her desire to donate known to close relatives. Although most people say they do not object to organ donation, fewer than 15 percent fill out donor cards. Overall, only 2 to 3 percent of donated organs are received as a result of donor cards. Ironically, those who fill out the cards statistically prove to be not only civic minded, but also cautious: they are less likely to become accident victims than those who are less concerned about others.

Even if an accident victim has signed a donor card, there is no guarantee that the person's organs will be used. To qualify for organ donation, the donor must die in a hospital while on life-support systems that keep oxygen-rich blood circulating through the organs. Since the life-support systems keep the heart beating after death, this is called brain death. The organs must be taken, or "harvested," after brain death occurs but before life support is turned off.

When brain death has occurred, hospitals require that a close relative must consent to the organ donation. When a close relative cannot be reached in time, the organs are lost even if a donor card has been signed. Someday, hospital policies may change so that the signature of relatives as witnesses on the donor card may assure that the wishes of the deceased are carried out.

Even when there is a signed donor card and the donor has died in a hospital, healthy organs are not always donated. The family may refuse to allow the organs to be donated. This is often because brain death is not completely understood and is not easily accepted by the family members. The deceased is warm and his or her heart is beating. It is hard for the family to believe there is no hope—that death has actually occurred. Sometimes organs that are vital to saving other lives begin to deteriorate before the family is able to accept brain death and grant permission for removal of the organs.

Grieving family members, especially anguished parents of young accident victims, do not usually think of donation on their own. Many of these precious organs will not be donated unless someone asks. Often a gentle reminder is all that is needed to give someone else's dying child a chance to live.

Requesting donation

Requesting the donation is a difficult task many would want to avoid. Yet, since organ donors are our only source of transplantable organs, asking is essential. In order to insure that families have the opportunity to donate, most states have passed "required request" laws. These laws require hospitals to request that every family consider donating the organs of their deceased loved ones. However, these laws are not enforced, and the request is not always made.

Requesting donation has become easier since

experience has proved that grieving families often welcome the opportunity to donate. To them, organ donation is an opportunity to bring something positive out of tragedy. In addition, most experts agree that donation helps the grieving family deal with their loss.

Most hospitals participate in the organ donation program today. The hospital staff person who asks for organ donations is specially trained in the best ways to approach grieving families. In smaller hospitals this person is usually a nurse but sometimes a minister or priest. Large hospitals have a procurement coordinator who handles a variety of activities, including obtaining permission from the donor's family for organ removal.

Once the family decides that it will allow a rel-

A surgical team performs a bone transplant in a child recipient.

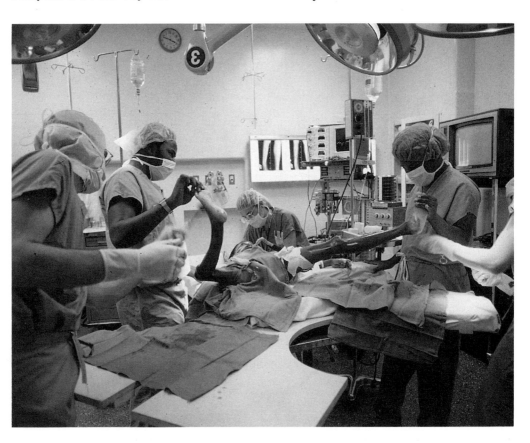

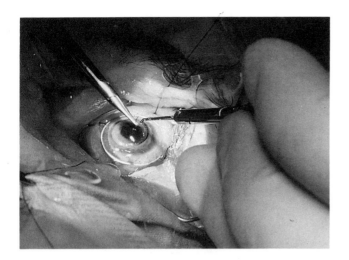

An eye surgeon sutures a donated cornea into the eye of a recipient. One person's body can provide many transplantable organs that can save or enhance the lives of many others.

ative to donate organs, the benefits are immense. One donor can save or greatly enhance the lives of as many as twenty-five recipients. One donor can provide one heart or four heart valves, two lungs, two kidneys, one liver, one pancreas, two hip joints, one jawbone, six ear bones, two corneas —plus limb bones, ribs, ligaments, tendons, cartilage, skin, and blood vessels.

Obviously, procuring more organs from potential donors is essential to saving the lives of many people. The problem of how to increase the supply of organs and who should receive the organs that are available, however, is fraught with ethical dilemmas. Researchers are constantly working to come up with new solutions, such as the development of artificial organs and the use of animal donors. At the same time, doctors work to find new ways to prevent diseases that attack organs and destroy them. Until these methods are perfected, doctors must continue to make life-and-death decisions regarding organ-transplant recipients.

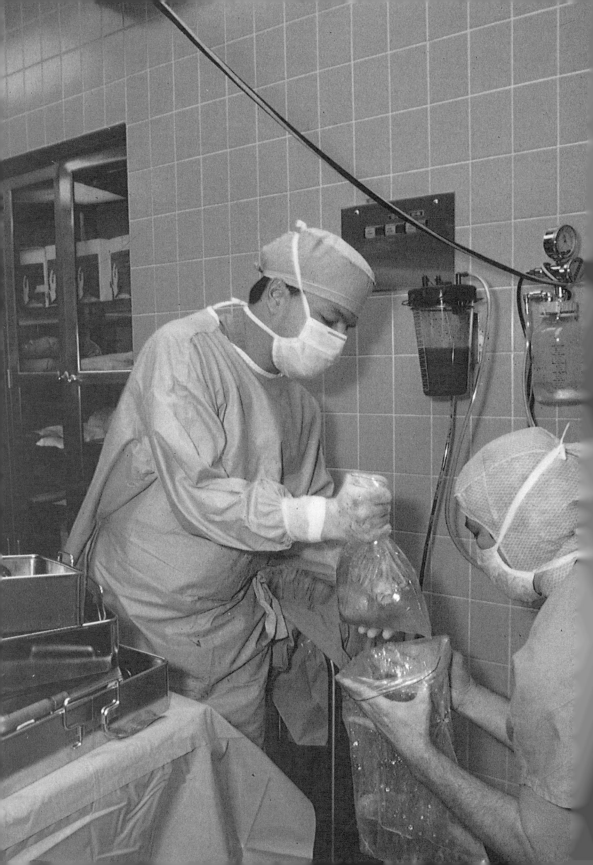

3

Ethical and Economic Considerations

THE NEED FOR DONOR ORGANS is far greater than the supply. The cold fact is there are not enough to go around. Some dying people will get a chance to live. Others will not. Decisions to determine who will get the organs are made in transplant centers every day. The guidelines for these decisions are set by UNOS policies, which are designed to assure that organs are distributed fairly. These policies forbid favoritism based on political influence, race, or sex.

The ethics committee

The need to fairly distribute limited medical resources has created a need for medical professionals dedicated to the study of standards of conduct and moral judgements, called medical ethicists. These medical ethicists study the difficult questions raised by the advances in organ transplantation and medical technology. Because of the increasing number of these questions, medical schools have created professorships and, in some cases, entire departments devoted to the study of ethics. The heads of these departments publish

(Opposite page) A transplant surgeon removes a donated heart from its cooler. The intended recipient of this organ is fortunate. The need for organs far exceeds the available supply.

49

Medical review boards have the unenviable task of setting the policies for choosing which patients receive a lifesaving transplant and which must continue to wait and hope.

their opinions on ethical issues in medical journals and newspapers. Doctors and hospital administrators use these opinions as guidelines for making difficult decisions and setting hospital policies. In addition, UNOS and many hospitals have their own ethics committees.

Almost anyone, including basketball players and plumbers, may serve on a hospital ethics committee. Usually the committee consists of doctors, nurses, ministers, social workers, and academic figures. It is desirable, however, to have a cross section of the community represented as well. Although committee members are volunteers, requirements for serving include a concern for the welfare of those who are ill, an interest in ethics, and a reputation for integrity and mature judgement.

The purpose of the ethics committee is to consider and assist in resolving unusual, complicated ethical problems that affect the care and treatment of patients. For example, members of the UNOS ethics committee offer opinions on the issue of anencephalic infants (those born missing most or all of the brain), including whether the organs should be donated, whether the organs are actually needed, and whether these infants should be declared brain dead. In hospitals that conduct research, the committee considers the ethics of experimental procedures on humans and/or animals. In these cases, the committee must decide whether the contribution to science is worth the pain and suffering of human and animal participants. For instance, in 1992, before the surgical team headed by Dr. Thomas Starzl transplanted a baboon liver into an unnamed man at the University of Pittsburgh, the ethics committee there had given its approval for up to four baboon-liver transplants in humans.

Living donors

Another ethical question that doctors and others struggle with is whether living donors should ever be used for transplants. With no immediate solution to the organ shortage in sight, some doctors encourage the use of living donors, usually a close relative of the recipient, in the case of a kidney or liver transplant. Desperate parents of young children whose lives hang in the balance are often eager to donate their own organs. For example, after waiting almost a year for a donor, Teresa Smith donated a portion of her own liver to save the life of her twenty-one-month-old daughter, Alyssa. A few days before the surgery, Teresa Smith was quoted in the *Los Angeles Times* as saying, "It was an obvious decision for me. Once you've given someone a big piece of your heart, it's easy to throw in a little bit of liver."

At the time of the surgery, Alyssa was 1 of 138

As dad John looks on, Teresa Smith kisses her baby Alyssa to whom she donated a segment of her own liver in an attempt to save the child's life.

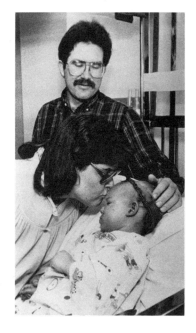

children age 5 or younger on the UNOS list waiting for a liver transplant. Due to the shortage of small donor organs, some transplant surgeons and ethicists endorsed use of the living liver donor. Transplants from living donors offer several advantages. For example, the surgery is scheduled, rather than performed as an emergency when the donor organ becomes available, and the donor and recipient can be HLA matched. In addition, there is a psychological benefit to the donor. If the transplant is successful, the donor has the satisfaction of having saved a relative's life. If it fails, the donor may be comforted in the knowledge that everything possible was done to save the life.

Some doctors, however, refuse to use living donors. In fact, Dr. Thomas Starzl, one of the pioneers in organ transplantation, stopped taking kidneys from living donors in 1972. Starzl said in an interview in *Omni* magazine, "When I did

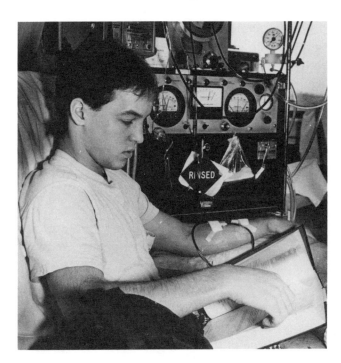

A college student studies while undergoing one of his thrice-weekly kidney dialysis treatments. Technology such as dialysis machines lessens the need for living donors to sacrifice a kidney for transplantation. The patient can undergo dialysis until a cadaver-donated organ is available.

those operations, I believed they were completely safe. But I later became aware of a number of deaths of kidney donors." Those deaths were not reported when they occurred, but the knowledge that there was in fact a risk to the donor was enough to discourage Dr. Starzl and others from using living donors. Technological advances have also made the need for living donors less urgent. Today kidney failure can be treated with dialysis and patients can often be kept alive until a cadaver donor can be found. With the ability to take organs from brain-dead cadavers and the discovery of cyclosporine, a transplanted cadaver organ is almost as likely to succeed as one from a living donor. Starzl and others therefore see little justification for taking kidneys from living people.

Many doctors also feel that living donors may not always be as willing to give up an organ as they seem. The family's concern for the desperately ill member may cause them to use excessive pressure to persuade likely donors to donate. Possible donors who refuse may be forever shunned by other members of the family.

Measuring risk

Surgeons and medical ethicists say that the risks to the donor from donating a portion of a liver are considerably higher than those of donating a kidney or bone marrow. Bone marrow is replaced in a matter of weeks, and the kidney donor is left with one undamaged kidney. However, no one has a second liver. If the liver is damaged when the donated portion is removed, the donor may die. For this reason, the University of Pittsburgh, a major pediatric liver transplant center, does not perform liver transplants from living donors. Dr. Ronald W. Busuttil of UCLA's transplant center supports this decision: "If I had a small child that needed a liver desperately, I would be able to find a [larger] donor and would cut down that liver before I would consider taking a segment of a relative's liver and putting it into the child."

Will the baby be a match?

Sometimes a search for a living donor goes even further. When no match is found among family members or the national registries, some parents have conceived an additional child, sometimes two, in an effort to provide a bone-marrow donor.

Although there is no competition for bone marrow and no line of waiting recipients, those who need bone-marrow transplants face a grave obstacle. They must find a perfect match. When the patient does not find a match among relatives, a search of the bone-marrow registries is the next best hope. Although there are over 500,000 willing donors listed with the National Marrow Donor Program (the largest registry), finding a match from non-relatives is rare. In fact, 70 percent of those desperately seeking a donor will not find one.

Abe and Mary Ayala were the first couple to publicly admit conceiving a child to serve as a bone-marrow donor. The baby, a girl they named Marissa, was a match for Anissa, their eighteen-year-old daughter, who was dying from leukemia. When Marissa was fourteen months old, she donated bone marrow to save her sister's life. A year later, Anissa showed no trace of leukemia.

Although there is little risk to a marrow donor, the Ayalas faced tremendous criticism when their story made the headlines. Some called it baby farming. Other skeptics used stronger terms, such as "cannibalizing of young children for spare parts." Dr. Robert Levine, an ethicist at Yale University's School of Medicine, found the idea trou-

A smiling Anissa Ayala holds her baby sister Marissa, who donated matching bone marrow to save Anissa from leukemia. The child was intentionally conceived by her parents to provide a donor to save Anissa's life.

Joined by his wife, Mary, and the transplant surgeon, Dr. Stephen Forman, Abe Ayala shows off his daughter Marissa at a press conference after she donated bone marrow for her leukemia-stricken older sister.

bling. "It seems to me that when a primary motive for conceiving a child is to produce tissue or an organ, we are getting very close to seeing this new being as a means to another end."

On the other hand, in a survey published in *Time* magazine, 47 percent of those who responded agreed with the Ayalas' decision. Dr. Norman Fost, a pediatrician and ethicist at the University of Wisconsin School of Medicine concurred. "Of all the reasons people have children, I think this is one of the better ones—to save a life," he said.

As for the Ayalas, they too saw it as a double opportunity: to save Anissa's life and have another child to love besides. As Mr. Ayala told a reporter a few months before the baby was born, "We just can't stand idly by and do nothing about it and wait for Anissa to die."

How many organs for one recipient?

The scarcity of organs causes many debates over organ transplants. Another controversial issue regarding scarcity is whether one very ill patient who needs several organs should be given precedence over several people who need just a single organ. This controversy was raised in December 1989 when a Pittsburgh transplant team led by Dr. Starzl transplanted a heart, liver, and kidney into one patient.

Dr. James F. Childless, a professor of religious studies and medical education at the University of Virginia, questioned this strategy: "Should three organs be used to save three lives or one?" With the success of multiple-organ transplants, other patients suffering from multiple-organ failure will certainly want transplants. As these patients seek multiple organs, the organ shortage will grow worse.

When an organ fails

The issue of how many organs one patient should receive also surfaces when a transplanted organ is rejected. When this occurs, the patient is re-listed. Since the organ rejection has usually left the patient close to death, the need for a replacement organ is urgent. UNOS places a patient whose body has rejected an organ high on the list. As a result, this patient may well get an organ that would have gone to someone else. Unfortunately, a second organ is not as likely to succeed as the first. Rejection is even more probable, due to antibodies formed in the rejection of the first organ.

Ethicists debate whether a patient who has already received and rejected one organ should get another while someone else on the list must continue to wait for a first organ. A spokesman for UNOS supports the current system, arguing that "if there is a reasonable chance of success, persons whose previous grafts failed should be given equal access to another." Dr. Childless agrees. He points out that while society may seek equitable distribution of scarce donor organs, doctors have always been taught not to abandon a patient. This means that once treatment has begun, doctors are obligated to continue it at all cost, even when one patient receives two or three organs while others die waiting.

Others are not so sure this direction is correct. Dr. George J. Annas, professor of health law at Boston University School of Public Health, insists that, "with a permanent shortage of organs, we must pay more attention to how the line is formed and who is next."

As long as transplanted organs can be rejected and people are dying for lack of donor organs, this debate will continue.

The economics of transplants

Even with the relative success of transplants, some argue that they are simply too expensive and should not be allowed. These critics contend that society should learn to accept death for the terminally ill and focus on preventive care for the healthy. If expensive treatments such as transplants were abandoned, these people believe, desperately needed services such as prenatal care for every expectant mother and preventive health care for children could be expanded. As Jeff Goldsmith, a health-care adviser, argues, "We have to rearrange how the dollars are being spent and refocus them on earlier stages of illness."

Americans already spend an astronomical amount on health care—about $800 billion in 1991—and the amount increases every year. Unless something is done to cut costs, the U.S. medical bill will double in the next ten years. Although efforts are being made to extend medical care to everyone our society cannot afford all the available treatments for everyone. As columnist Joseph P. Shapiro pointed out in a report in *U.S. News & World Report*, in any plan to reform

TRANSPLANTATION COSTS (1988)

	Kidney	Heart	Liver	Heart-Lung	Pancreas
Hospital Charges	$21,214	$62,463	$104,049	$98,127	$39,997
Professional Fees — Surgeon	$4,078	$10,000	$15,000	$16,553	$8,697
Professional Fees — Other	$2,043	$6,529	$10,466	$8,173	$2,823
Donor-Organ Acquisition	$12,290	$12,578	$16,281	$12,028	$15,400
TOTALS	$39,625	$91,570	$145,795	$134,881	$66,917

Source: Battelle-Seattle Research Center, Seattle, Washingtonn.

health care, "it will be hard to balance limited health-care resources and claims for equal treatment."

No doubt, organ transplants are among the most expensive medical procedures. The costs reported for solid organ transplant surgery in 1988 range from $25,000, the lowest figure for a kidney transplant, to $230,000 for the most expensive liver transplant. In addition to the cost of the surgery, drugs to prevent rejection are almost always necessary. The cost can be as much as $10,000 per year, or even more.

Most people cannot afford an organ transplant without financial assistance. As a result, the federal government shoulders much of the financial burden, along with state governments and private insurance.

If a person who needs a transplant does not have medical insurance, Medicare, or cash, he or she will not be listed on the waiting list for an organ transplant by most transplant centers. The patient must either raise the money or face the consequences of the illness. As Ronald Milhorn, a policy analyst with the Health Care Financing Administration, noted in *Business Week*, "The alternative to a liver transplant is death, and death is cheaper." For many—those who make too much money to qualify for Medicaid and not enough to afford insurance—the only hope lies in fund-raisers and public appeals for donations.

Some complain that the present system of organ distribution is not fair. Those without money often cannot be listed at all. Patients with enough money can increase their chances of getting an organ by paying to have themselves listed through more than one transplant center.

"The growing conflict between economics and ethics may be the most serious challenge to medicine's future," writes Edmund D. Pellegrino, M.D., in the *Journal of the American Medical Association*. This seems especially true for organ transplants, one of the most expensive medical treatments. Although even an unlimited supply of money could not buy a transplant for everyone who needs one because of organ scarcity, the issue of which medical procedures should be pursued will remain hotly contested.

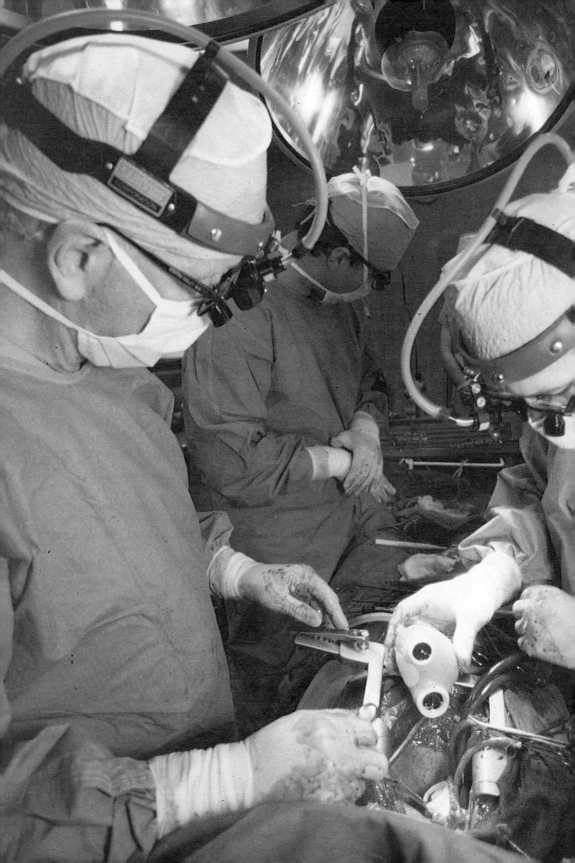

4

Solutions to the Organ Shortage

OUT OF THE MORE than 2,000,000 people who die in the United States each year, only 10,700 at most meet the current criteria for organ donation—that is, they are healthy, within the acceptable age range, and die while on life support in a hospital. Since thousands of people need organs each year, the 10,700 possible donors could not eliminate the organ shortage even if every possible donor agreed to donate organs upon his or her death. This fact has caused doctors, researchers, and scientists to search for other possible solutions. Some of these proposals have raised controversies that may prevent or at least slow their widespread adoption.

Encouraging consent

(Opposite page) While technology and experience have made heart and other organ transplants almost routine, a shortage of usable organs remains a problem. The Jarvik-7, pictured here, has been used as a temporary lifeline for patients waiting for a donor heart.

Until these controversies can be overcome, the most immediate way to increase the organ supply is still to obtain consent from all possible donors. This alone could double the number of organs available each year. As Robert M. Veatch, Ph.D., director of the Kennedy Institute of Ethics, writes, "Many things could and should be done to maximize the likelihood of actual consent." In fact, UNOS and the Coalition on Donation believe that the first step toward this goal may be to promote organ donation. As Dr. James S. Wolf, chairman of the coalition, has said, "We want to convince each and every person that donation is a social responsibility . . . the right thing to do." He hopes that with increased awareness, organ donation will become widely accepted, a lifesaving action as common as buckling a seat belt or not smoking.

Another way to increase awareness and make organ donation more routine would be for doctors to make the subject a part of every medical history and physical examination. Or a consent form could be added to the driver's license renewal form or to income-tax forms. As Dr. Veatch says, "It seems little to ask for what could be a lifesaving decision."

Expanding the donor pool

Another possible solution to the inadequate donor pool is to expand the criteria for acceptable donors. This has already been done with some criteria such as age. At one time no one over the age of 45 could donate organs. Today, healthy organs are accepted from donors up to age 70. The donor pool has been further expanded to include people whose organs are healthy although they have minor health problems. Many physicians believe that even more of the restrictions that limit the donor pool must be lifted. Some believe the use of older and even imperfect organs would save lives.

These imperfect organs have already been used with some success. James Taylor, for example, was in urgent need of a donor heart. As the sixty-eight-year-old man's condition worsened, no heart became available. In order to save Taylor's life, doctors at UCLA Medical Center in California decided to use a donor heart that needed re-

pair and normally would not have been used because of clogged arteries. Veins from Taylor's legs were used to replace the arteries. James Taylor received the repaired heart and was reported in good condition after the transplant. According to Taylor's physician, "The heart has worked beautifully."

Another possibility for increasing the donor pool is to accept organs from donors who did not die on life support. Organs that could be used from these non-heartbeating donors include the kidneys. Kidneys can be preserved for a few hours after the heart stops beating. A catheter is slipped through a small incision in the groin to carry a cold solution to the kidneys. This cooling prevents damage to the organs long enough to obtain consent from the next of kin for the donation. Although currently these donors are not routinely used, some people, including Lawrence Hopkins,

The gloved hands of a transplant specialist ready a kidney for transplantation. The number of kidneys available for transplantation would be greatly increased if suitability requirements for donated organs were less rigid.

director of operations at the Regional Organ Bank of Illinois, believe they could significantly increase the number of available kidneys. He estimates that "through the use of non-heartbeating cadaveric donors, we could potentially procure kidneys from an extra 150 donors a year" in Illinois alone.

Presumed consent

Another method of increasing the donor pool is to change the laws concerning consent. As it now stands, U.S. law goes to great lengths to carry out the wishes of the deceased and his or her family. Consent is required before organs can be removed for donation. Many, including Dr. Aaron Spital of the University of Maryland, believe that changing this law would greatly increase the number of organ donors.

Some European countries, for example, have adopted "presumed consent" laws to increase the number of donors. These laws assume that everyone wants to donate. Unless the deceased has filed an objection or the family protests, organs are routinely procured from cadavers. Belgium adopted a system of presumed consent in 1986. By 1991 the number of transplanted organs had increased by 140 percent. Advocates believe this method could work in the United States as well.

Dr. Robert M. Veatch of the Kennedy Institute of Ethics counters that the presumed consent change may not increase organ donation. He writes that "the same family members who object to transplantation when asked will still object under a presumed-consent law." Those who agree with this view believe that the only increase in donor organs likely to result from presumed consent would be those organs that are now lost because the family cannot be reached in time to give consent.

Presumed consent laws would still allow those with objections to refuse to donate organs. However, it would weight a decision in favor of donating, since a potential donor or relatives would have to *decide* not to donate. The fact that consent would be presumed might also eventually lead to greater familiarity with and thus acceptance of the idea among the general public.

Paying for organs

Some in the medical profession suggest further changes in the system that are more controversial. One of these plans is to pay the next of kin, the person who is legally responsible for giving permission for the donation. This solution is controversial because it is so different from the current

"I will do your gallstones and your wife's broken pelvis for your left kidney."

procedure. No payment is ever given to the donor or the donor's family. Buying or selling organs is, in fact, illegal.

But some insist that the current system of voluntary donation has not produced enough organs from the potential supply. Dr. Thomas C. Peters of the Jacksonville Transplant Center in Florida has suggested studying the possibility of a one-time payment of $1,000 to the donor family. Another possibility is covering burial expenses for the organ donor. Still another suggestion is for the payment to be set up in a life-insurance policy. The donor's beneficiaries would receive payment after the organs were donated. Because paying for organs is illegal, these payments would not be offered as payment for the organs but in return for the family's decision to donate.

Although this measure might save lives, almost any suggestion of paying a death benefit to increase donation brings immediate protests. Some feel that a death benefit may coerce family members to donate a deceased member's organs out of economic interest. Others think that offering payment for organs would dishonor the deceased as well as donors of the past. "The body is not an object to be scavenged," ethicist Dr. Pellegrain of the Center for the Advanced Study of Ethics at Georgetown University insists, "[not] even for good purposes."

Procuring organs from anencephalic infants

Another solution to the organ shortage debated on legal and moral grounds is that of altering brain-death laws to allow organ donation from anencephalic infants.

Anencephalic infants are born with little or no brain tissue, only a brain stem. Since the brain stem controls automatic body functions, these babies breathe, have a heartbeat, jump at loud noises, suck, and blink. They cannot think or reason. In most cases, anencephalic babies live no more than a few days. Many parents of anencephalic infants would like to make something good come out of their tragedy by donating their baby's organs. However, the law states that brain death has occurred when all brain activity has ceased. Since these babies have brain-stem activity, they cannot be considered brain dead under the current legal definition.

Baby Theresa

One heartrending case involved Baby Theresa, born March 21, 1992, at Broward General Medical Center in Fort Lauderdale, Florida. Theresa was diagnosed as anencephalic months before birth. Her parents decided to donate her organs. Baby Theresa's parents asked the Florida courts to declare Theresa dead at birth so her organs could be donated. Their request was denied. Baby Theresa died when she was nine days old. By that time her organs had sustained damage and could not be transplanted.

Dr. Roger Evans, senior research scientist at Battelle-Seattle Research Center, finds the loss of such organs unacceptable. He argues that "we must balance the lives of the anencephalic and the three to five people waiting for transplant." In other words, we should weigh the good of saving lives against the brain-death law that prevents the use of such organs. To Dr. Evans, not using the organs from anencephalic infants "is an obvious waste."

Steven Gundry, M.D., of Loma Linda Medical Center agrees. "The women who choose to carry an anencephalic child . . . feel that the child's ultimate demise could mean saving three to four children." Although these parents suffer a great loss, they want to give a tremendous gift. Dr.

Gundry and others feel they should be allowed to do so.

Others object to altering the definition of death to include anencephalic infants. Some fear this step might lead to further alterations in the definition of death to include the severely retarded, people in comas, or those suffering from Alzheimer's disease. Some find it very disturbing that a lawyer went to court to ask that Baby Theresa be declared dead in direct defiance of the brain-death law. Dr. Robert Veatch is one professional who holds this view: "You can't make a person brain dead by judicial decree. By the present definition of death, this baby was not dead. . . . Its brain stem was functioning."

Still others believe that the anencephalic-infant issue is distracting and counterproductive. The most needed organ from the anencephalic infant is the heart. The other organs are often too small or immature to transplant successfully. Because of this, Dr. Jeremiah Turcotte of the Transplant and Health Policy Center in Ann Arbor, Michigan, discourages further argument over anencephalic infants, noting that altering brain-death laws is a very complex matter, while the use of these organs does not offer a substantial solution to the organ shortage. He says, "Anencephalic infants are not a practical source of a significant number of organs."

Animal donors

Other solutions may prove more practical but may not be easily accepted by the general public. One that many doctors, including Leonard Bailey of Loma Linda University and Thomas Starzl of the University of Pittsburgh, have explored is cross-species transplantation, or using the organs of animals. Although the difference in tissue types between species makes controlling rejection more difficult, some doctors see the cross-species transplant, or xenograft, as the sole way to solve the organ shortage.

On the other hand, many people question the ethics of killing an animal so that a human can live. Several well-publicized cases have brought this issue into the spotlight. On October 26, 1984, Dr. Leonard Bailey transplanted a baboon's heart into Baby Fae. She was twelve days old. Baby Fae, born with hypoplastic left heart syndrome, would have died within two days. With the baboon heart, she lived twenty days, longer than anyone else with a cross-species heart transplant. People who objected to the transplant point out that Baby Fae had very little chance of long-term survival. They argue that it was ethically wrong

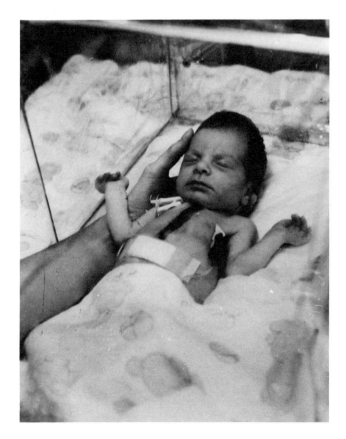

Baby Fae received the heart of a baboon. She lived twenty days after the transplant.

to kill an animal for what amounted to an unjustified experiment.

Eight years later, on June 29, 1992, a surgical team headed by Dr. Thomas Starzl transplanted a baboon liver into a human. The patient, whose name was withheld, suffered from hepatitis B and AIDS. He was not eligible for a donated human liver because the hepatitis B virus would have attacked a transplanted human liver. The baboon liver, however, was thought to be immune to this virus. Unfortunately, the man suffered a brain hemorrhage and died before this theory could be proved. At the time of death there was no evidence of organ rejection. He survived ten weeks with a cross-species transplant.

Another attempt to transplant an animal organ into a human was made in October 1992. Dr. Leonard Makowka and his transplant team at Cedars-Sinai Hospital in Los Angeles transplanted a pig liver into a twenty-four-year-old woman named Susan Fowler. The transplant was intended to be a temporary measure to keep the woman alive until a human liver could be found. Although a human liver was found, the woman died before it could be transplanted.

Bailey, Starzl, and Makowka made extreme attempts to save their dying patients when no human organs were available. For them it was a risk worth taking—the only hope to save a life. The doctors also saw a future benefit: information from these cross-species transplants may one day contribute to a solution to the critical shortage of transplantable organs.

Others vehemently disagree with the doctors' logic. Many animal protection groups would like to halt all research and human surgery that involves animals. Suzanne E. Roy, public affairs director of the animal rights group In Defense of Animals, argues that the animal kingdom should not become "spare parts supply houses for humankind." She says that causing a lot of animal suffering for unknown human benefit is "science without ethics."

Implantable mechanical organs

In addition to animal organs, other alternatives to human organs are being sought. For example, scientists have been working on a mechanical heart since the early 1960s. Unfortunately, the more they try, the more scientists realize what a poor substitute such a machine is for the human organ. For the most part the challenge has been too great, since a successful implant must be small enough to be implanted completely inside the body with its own power supply; it must last the life of the patient; and the patient's blood must not clot on the inside surfaces of the device.

On December 2, 1982, Barney Clark became famous as the first of five volunteers to receive the Jarvik-7, the first artificial heart. He lived 112 days. During this time the artificial heart proved to be far less desirable than a human heart. The major disadvantage was that blood clots formed in the pumping chamber. As these clots broke

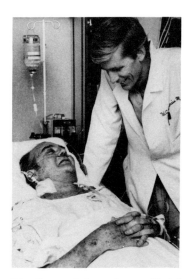

The first recipient of an artificial heart, Barney Clark smiles wanly at surgeon William DeVries.

away and traveled to the brain, Barney Clark suffered numerous strokes. None of the other volunteers fared any better. As a result, use of the Jarvik-7 as a permanent artificial heart was abandoned. It has, however, been used as a temporary lifeline for more than ninety patients waiting for a donor heart. Research continues, although it is controversial.

Benefits of the artificial heart

A study conducted by the University of Washington School of Public Health and Community Medicine drew some conclusions about the prospects of pursuing the artificial heart. In it, the panel concluded that research in the artificial heart should continue. Although so far unsuccessful on a long-term basis, the device offers hope of prolonging life for thousands of heart-disease patients who would otherwise die. By the year 2010 the artificial heart is expected to keep an average user alive almost four-and-a-half years—at a cost of about $105,000 per patient per year.

In the same study, the panel concluded that the artificial heart would cost more and be less beneficial than any other medical treatment now in use, including heart transplants. The U.S. government has already spent more than $260 million on research that has not produced an efficient artificial heart. (The Jarvik-7 was privately funded.)

Opponents of the artificial heart, such as Claude Lenfant, director of the National Heart, Lung, and Blood Institute, think it is too expensive. "The country is going to have quite a burden if it has to take care of 150,000 people with an artificial heart."

Mechanical replacements for other organs are not even on the drawing board. Size is the first obstacle. For example, some estimate than an artificial liver would be a chemical plant covering

The Jarvik-7 failed as a permanent replacement for a natural heart, but has been successful as a temporary bridge to keep patients alive until a donor heart can be found.

anywhere from several acres to six square miles. Cost, of course, is another drawback.

Although mechanical organs are not yet an option for those who wait for a donor organ, other possibilities are being studied. Researchers are using all the tools of medical science to come up with replacements for organs such as the liver, lungs, and pancreas. Ideas that seem to be far-out science fiction today may in a few years become as common as hip replacements are now.

5

The Future

ALTHOUGH TODAY'S transplant surgeons have an arsenal of anti-rejection drugs at their command, the search for the ideal drug continues. With a combination of cyclosporine and other drugs, most rejection can be controlled and usually reversed should it occur. Unpleasant side effects to the drugs remain, however, and doctors would like to make life after the transplant better for the patient.

One drug now being tested on humans is very promising. FK-506, made by Japan's Fujisawa Pharmaceutical Company, may prove to be one hundred times as powerful as cyclosporine. In clinical tests, FK-506 produced fewer side effects than cyclosporine and seemed to be particularly effective in preventing liver rejection. Like cyclosporine, FK-506 was found in soil. It prevents rejection by preventing lymphocytes, or white blood cells, from attacking transplanted organs. FK-506 has been tested in more than one hundred organ recipients. Late in 1989 Dr. Keith Johnson, clinical director of renal transplantation at Vanderbilt University in Nashville, said: "We're hoping that this is the magic medicine." FK-506 was also considered to have been a major factor in preventing rejection in the case of the baboon-liver transplant in 1992. The ten-week survival

(Opposite page) A heart transplant recipient walks as part of an exercise program to keep himself and his new heart healthy.

75

time of this transplant patient offers hope that FK-506 may indeed be a magic medicine. It may help to make cross-species transplants more routine.

Genetic engineering

Genetic engineering offers another possibility for improved immunosuppressive drugs through a technique called gene splicing. In this technique microscopic fragments of selected genetic material from one cell are transferred to another. The second cell then acquires the characteristics of the first. As the cell multiplies, new cells have the combined characteristics of the parent cells. One genetically engineered antibody, CTLA4Ig, now being tested in mice, may prove effective in controlling organ rejection and infection and may be useful in cross-species transplants as well. In clinical tests, twelve diabetic mice were implanted with human pancreas tissue and then treated with CTLA4Ig. One hundred days later the mice showed no signs of rejection and no symptoms of diabetes. The biggest benefit to this drug is that it only affects the portion of the immune system that attacks the transplanted organ. The rest of the immune system remains undamaged and able to fight infection.

Custom designed HLA molecules

Genetic engineering techniques also offer the possibility of expanding the acceptance of human and animal organs. In the future, it may be possible to genetically engineer, or alter, the antigens on the surface of HLA molecules. As a result, someday HLA molecules on donor-organ cells may be custom designed to provide a perfect match for each recipient. Scientists may also be able to remove the HLA antigens altogether. The new genetically engineered organs would have no antigens to trigger the immune response. Any organ, including organs from animals, would be acceptable to any recipient. Either process would eliminate rejection and the need for anti-rejection drugs.

Discovering new ways to control the immune system

In addition to new drugs, scientists are discovering more ways to control the immune system. While performing heart transplants on mice, for example, researchers in Japan and the United States made a fascinating discovery about how the immune system works. These scientists determined that adhesion molecules, a dozen sticky proteins that act as a glue to hold cells together, play a significant role in the early stages of the immune response. Before the T cells (lymphocytes) leap into action, an adhesion molecule on the T cell surface must stick to an adhesion molecule on the surface of a cell from the foreign tissue. Once the two adhesion molecules join, the connection is complete—like closing an electric circuit. In a flash the T cell receives a signal that identifies the cell as foreign. The rejection process begins immediately.

These scientists have found that custom-designed antibodies will block the joining of the adhesion molecules. As a result, the T cells cannot identify the transplanted organ as foreign and the rejection process is prevented. Researchers injected specially constructed antibodies into the mice at the time of the heart transplants to prevent rejection. They found that the antibodies did not damage the T cells. After a few weeks, they seem to disappear completely from the system. Moreover, for reasons not yet fully understood, the transplanted organ is permanently safe from rejection.

Since the immune system of mice is different

from that of humans, more trials are needed. Yet, someday these experiments could lead to the elimination of organ rejection in human transplant patients.

Preserving donated organs

Another important problem researchers are trying to solve has to do with extending the amount of time donor organs can be preserved before being transplanted. The present four-to-six-hour limit on a donor heart, for example, means that recipient and donor must be within a thousand miles of each other. Lengthening the time the donor heart can be ischemic, without blood circulating through it, could vastly improve the transplant process. Longer preservation would allow more time for HLA matching and transportation of the organs. In effect, more time for HLA

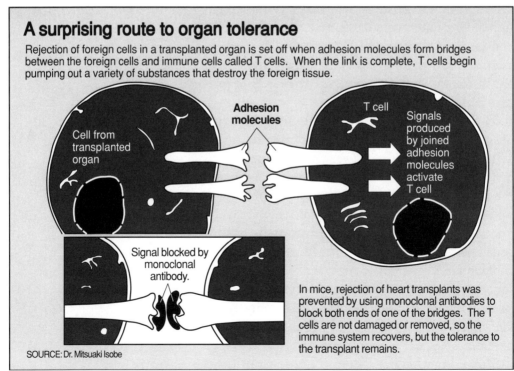

A surprising route to organ tolerance

Rejection of foreign cells in a transplanted organ is set off when adhesion molecules form bridges between the foreign cells and immune cells called T cells. When the link is complete, T cells begin pumping out a variety of substances that destroy the foreign tissue.

Cell from transplanted organ

Adhesion molecules

T cell

Signals produced by joined adhesion molecules activate T cell

Signal blocked by monoclonal antibody.

In mice, rejection of heart transplants was prevented by using monoclonal antibodies to block both ends of one of the bridges. The T cells are not damaged or removed, so the immune system recovers, but the tolerance to the transplant remains.

SOURCE: Dr. Mitsuaki Isobe

matching could reduce organ rejection and fewer patients would need second and third transplants. More time would also allow a closer size and age match to take place—especially for the very young, where size counts the most.

A fish, the Newfoundland ocean pout, may hold the key to preserving organs. According to Boris Rabinsky, a professor of biomedical engineering at the University of California at Berkeley, certain proteins protect the fish from seasonal changes in water temperature by acting something like an antifreeze. In experiments with the fish proteins, researchers were able to preserve rat livers for as long as twenty-four hours. Early experiments indicate these proteins may also extend the time human organs can be stored for transplantation.

Organs from the laboratory

While many improvements focus on increasing the present organ supply, in the future scientists hope to be able to create replacement organs from cell cultures. In a process known as "tissue engineering," biomedical researchers can grow living tissue in the laboratory. The cells grow in laboratory containers filled with a special nutrient mixture. Scientists have successfully used this technique to grow skin as well as other organ tissues.

These manufactured living tissues are similar to natural tissue but not identical. For example, the skin equivalent does not have pigment and will not grow hair.

Skin equivalent, the first manufactured human organ, is designed to be used as a permanent skin replacement for burn victims. Like natural skin, the skin equivalent acts as a protective shield to keep infection out and hold the fluids in the tissue. Early tests have proved successful, and the company plans to have the product on the market by 1993.

Transplant surgeons prepare to harvest the organs of a brain dead accident victim. The organs will then be placed in the coolers and rushed to nearby transplant centers.

Encouraged by the success of skin equivalent, Organogenesis and several other companies are working to produce other organ and tissue equivalents. For example, Organogenesis has begun testing a blood vessel equivalent, which is designed to replace clogged and damaged arteries. This would be useful in heart bypass surgery to replace coronary arteries, as well as to replace cerebral arteries in stroke victims. In addition, blood vessel equivalent may prove useful in replacing damaged arteries in diseased or injured legs and arms. Other companies are researching an artificial bone marrow. Some progress has been made in producing stem cells that may be used for bone-marrow transplants or as natural killer cells for treating cancer in the future.

The tissue engineering process has great potential for other organs as well. Small masses of liver cells have been grown and implanted into animals. These manufactured liver cells have been able to survive and produce a variety of proteins and enzymes normally produced in the liver. Work is in progress to produce thyroid, cartilage, and tissue for replacing or repairing intestinal and urinary tracts as well.

This work in manufactured tissues offers hope for an alternative to human donor organs and one possible solution to the organ shortage.

Bionic organs

Bionic, or mechanical, organs are another experimental alternative to human donor organs. Currently, the only promising bionic vital organ is the heart. As a result of the failure to produce an efficient artificial heart, research is focused on producing a temporary device to keep heart patients alive until a donor heart becomes available. The most promising of these, the battery-powered Heart-Mate, received Food and Drug Administration

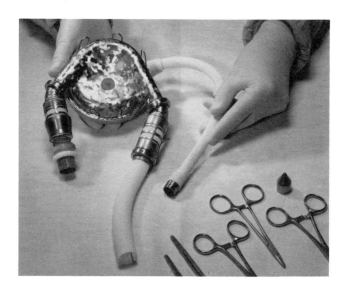

New technology such as this HeartMate pumping device gives greater hope to patients waiting for donated hearts.

(FDA) approval for clinical trials in January 1991.

The HeartMate pumping chamber is implanted in the chest just under the diaphragm; however, it is powered by two 1½-pound lead-acid batteries worn outside the body in a specially designed shoulder harness. Freshly charged batteries last eight to ten hours. When the batteries weaken, an alarm sounds. At night, the HeartMate is switched from batteries to a bedside console. So far three patients have received the HeartMate in clinical trials. Two died of unrelated causes and a third, thirty-three-year-old Michael Templeton, is alive and well, still waiting for a donor heart. His size, more than 220 pounds before his illness, has made finding a donor heart more difficult; the HeartMate made it less urgent. With the heart Templeton can move about and exercise. As a result, he has actually grown stronger while waiting for a donor heart.

Someday heart-assist devices like HeartMate may be used routinely to keep heart patients alive and well until a donor heart becomes available.

Other heart-assist devices under development include the Bio-pump, a centrifugal pump that is

Texan Michael Templeton holds a heart pump similar to the one surgeons implanted in his body to assist his damaged heart until a donor can be found.

PULSATILE PUMP

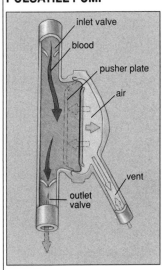

Some pump designs plagiarize nature's method: A collecting chamber contracts each time it fills with blood, forcing the blood through a one-way valve to the arteries. Thermo Cardiosystem's HeartMate pump, for example, has a flat disc that pushes forward to expel the blood. Each time the pump "contracts," air from an outside vent rushes into the expanding pocket behind the disc to prevent a vacuum from forming.

CENTRIFUGAL PUMP

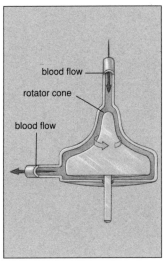

A different approach is to move blood continuously, instead of in short bursts. The Bio-pump by Medtronic Bio-Medicus of Minneapolis spins a smooth, conical rotor in blood-filled chamber. The centrifugal force draws the blood out the exit tube in an even flow. "We don't think it makes a difference physiologically whether we use pulsatile pumps or continuous-flow ones," remarks Steve Parnis, a senior researcher at the Texas Heart Institute. The Bio-Medicus system is not implanted; blood circulates between the patient's body and a console via connecting hoses.

ROTOR PUMP

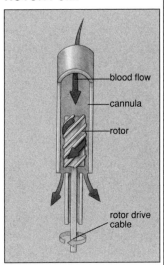

Continuous-flow pumps can be much smaller because there are no chambers and valves. That's the strategy of the Hemopump, made by Johnson and Johnson Interventional Systems Co. in Edison, N.J. Surgeons insert the Hemopump, which resembles a tiny drill bit, into a major artery, such as in the leg. Using fluoroscopy, surgeons then steer the Hemopump through the body and into the left ventricle where the device whirls at 25,000 rpm. It propels up to three liters of blood per minute, less than half the capacity of the HeartMate.

not implanted inside the body. Tubes connect the patient to the device, which is held in a bedside console. Blood circulates from the patient to the device, where the blood is moved in a continuous flow by a smooth, cone-shaped rotor that spins in a blood-filled chamber. Circulation from the patient's heart is boosted as the blood flows through the chamber and back to the body. Another device, the Hemopump, is a rotor pump that looks like a tiny drill bit. It is inserted into a major artery, usually in the leg. Viewing the procedure on a fluoroscope, surgeons guide the Hemopump through the artery to the left ventricle of the heart. There the device whirls at 25,000 rpm to assist the heart in pumping blood throughout the body.

The search for a permanent solution

The drawback to these devices is that they are *temporary,* and so do nothing to ease the donor-organ shortage. In fact, they have the potential to increase the demand. The ultimate goal of researchers is a permanent heart-assist device that would serve as an alternative to human donor organs. Power for such a device might travel through unbroken skin from batteries worn in a belt around the waist. This would eliminate the danger of infection, which is a major threat when the power source is connected to the device by wires that pierce the skin.

Even with all of these futuristic solutions, however, doctors such as Dr. Thomas Starzl believe that "transplantation will remain the nuclear component in the spare-parts field and won't be replaced by artificial organs." Instead, as Starzl looks to the future, he predicts that "the next stage of transplanting will almost certainly be xenografting—animal to man."

So far, organ transplantation can be viewed as one of the most remarkable success stories in medical history. Although many hurdles remain ahead, without doubt, a new generation of scientists will not accept the shortage of donor organs as defeat. They will continue in their search to discover how to meet the demand.

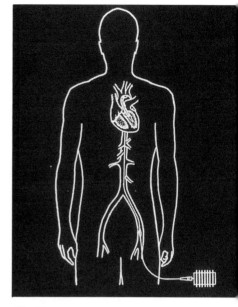

The Hemopump is inserted in a large artery in the leg and guided into the left ventricle of the heart where it helps the organ pump blood more efficiently.

Glossary

anastomosis: A surgical technique for joining blood vessels or intestines together.

anesthesia: A chemical that deadens nerves or causes the loss of consciousness to prevent a patient from feeling pain; can be local, limited to a certain area; or general, where the patient loses consciousness.

antibodies: Proteins produced by the leukocytes (white blood cells) when they come in contact with antigens of foreign cells. Antibodies are custom designed by the white blood cells to destroy specific foreign cells.

antigens: Molecules on the surface of cells that trigger the immune response.

anti-rejection drugs: Drugs that fight against rejection of foreign bodies or tissue.

autotransplant: A transplant from one part of the same body to another.

azathioprine: A drug used to kill multiplying cancer cells. Because lymphocytes (white blood cells made by lymphatic tissue) are similar to cancer cells, azathioprine also kills lymphocytes and is used to suppress the immune system in transplant patients.

beating-heart cadaver: A brain-dead cadaver whose blood is kept circulating by life-support machines until organs can be removed.

biopsy: Removal of a sliver of living tissue for examination under a microscope to look for evidence of disease or organ rejection.

cadaver: A dead body.

cardiovascular: The heart and blood vessels; the circulatory system.

dialysis: Cleansing the blood of a patient with an artificial-kidney machine.

donor: One whose organs are donated for transplant; may be living or cadaver.

ethics: Moral convictions that distinguish right from wrong.

gene splicing: The technology of taking a microscopic fragment of one cell and inserting it into another to change the genetic characteristics of the second cell.

HLA: Human leukocyte antigens, which identify every cell in the human body as either its own or foreign.

human leukocyte antigens: See HLA.

immune response: The immune system's attack on foreign cells.

immune system: The body's defense against disease and foreign invaders.

immunologist: Specialist in the immune system.

immunosuppression: Making certain antibodies inactive to permit the body's acceptance of a foreign substance, such as a transplanted organ.

immunosuppressive drugs: Drugs that suppress the immune system.

ischemic: Without blood. Also refers to the time a donor organ can be out of the body.

leukocyte: A white blood cell.

lymphocyte: White blood cell made by lymphatic tissue; T cells are made by the thymus, B cells are made in the bone marrow.

organ rejection: The body's natural defense system's attack on the transplanted organ.

registrant: A person whose name is on the United Network for Organ Sharing registry as waiting for an organ.

solid organs: Organs as such as heart, kidney, liver, pancreas, and lung.

steroids: Chemical relatives of hormones made by the human adrenal gland, such as cortisone and prednisone, which suppress the immune system.

survival rates: The percent of people who survive a certain length of time after transplant; 20 percent would mean twenty out of one hundred survived for the given time.

sutures: Stitches that hold a surgical incision together.

tissue match: To find tissues with the same HLA molecules.

UNOS: United Network for Organ Sharing—an organization established by the federal government to oversee the distribution of donor organs. All patients eligible for a donor organ are listed with UNOS.

xenograft: Transplants between species, such as from a dog to a goat or from a baboon to a human.

Organizations
to Contact

The following organizations provide services or information about organ transplants. The addresses and phone numbers when available are provided so more information can be obtained directly from each organization.

American Transplant Association
PO Box 822123
Dallas, TX 75382-2123
(214) 340-0942

Children's Transplant Association
PO Box 53699
Dallas, TX 75253
(214) 287-8484

National Kidney Foundation, Inc.
30 E. 33rd St.
New York, NY 10016
(800) 622-9010

**National Marrow Donor Program
Coordinating Center**
3433 Broadway NE, Suite 400
Minneapolis, MN 55413
(800) 654-1247
(612) 627-5865

**Regional Organ Procurement Agency
of Southern California**
950 Veteran Ave.
Los Angeles, CA 90024
(213) 825-7651

Transplant Recipients International Organization (TRIO)
244 N. Bellefield Ave.
Pittsburgh, PA 15213
(412) 687-2210

United Network for Organ Sharing (UNOS)
1100 Boulders Parkway, Suite 500
PO Box 13770
Richmond, VA 23225-8770
(800) 24-DONOR
(803) 330-8500

In addition, the author recommends the following newsletters:

Chance of a Lifetime
For the volunteers who make miracles happen
PO Box 18130
Minneapolis, MN 55413

UNOS Update
1100 Boulders Parkway, Suite 500
PO Box 13770
Richmond, VA 23225-8770

Suggestions for Further Reading

Lawrence K. Altman, "New Drug Boosts Transplant Odds," *Reader's Digest*, February 1990.

Dr. Christiaan Barnard and Curtis Bill Pepper, *One Life*. New York: Macmillan, 1969.

S. Rickly Christian, *A Gift of Life*. San Bernardino, CA: Here's Life Publishers, 1986.

Mark Dowie, *We Have a Donor: The Bold New World of Organ Transplanting*. New York: St. Martin's Press, 1988.

William H. Frist, *Transplant: A Heart Surgeon's Account of the Life-and-Death Dramas of the New Medicine*. New York: The Atlantic Monthly Press, 1989.

Christine Gorman, "Matchmaker, Find Me a Match," *Time*, June 17, 1991.

Lee Gutkind, *Many Sleepless Nights*. New York: W.W. Norton & Co., 1988.

Eric Lax, *Life and Death on 10 West*. New York: Times Books, 1984.

Gerald Leinwand, *Transplants, Today's Medical Miracles*. New York: Franklin Watts, 1977.

Theodore I. Malinin, *Surgery and Life: The Extraordinary Career of Alexis Carrel*. New York: Harcourt Brace Jovanovich, 1979.

Lance Morrow, "When One Body Can Save Another," *Time*, June 17, 1991.

Judith Anne Yeaple, "The Bionic Heart," *Popular Science*, April 1992.

Works Consulted

Lawrence K. Altman, "The Limits of Transplantation: How Far Should Surgeons Go?" *The New York Times*, December 19, 1989.

John Antczak, "Pig's Liver Implanted to Keep Woman Alive," *The San Diego Union-Tribune*, October 13, 1992.

Sandra Blakeslee, "Mouse Transplant Results Surprise Doctors," *The San Diego Union-Tribune*, March 18, 1992.

Sandra Blakeslee, "Quandaries of Timing on Infant Organs," *The New York Times*, February 23, 1988.

Sandra Blakeslee, "Studies Find Unequal Access to Kidney Transplants," *The New York Times*, January 29, 1989.

Carol Bolotin, "Drug as a Hero," *Science*, June 1985.

Arthur Caplan, "Ethical Issues Raised by Research Involving Xenografts," *Journal of the American Medical Association*, December 20, 1985.

Arthur Caplan, "Transplanted Pig Liver Is a Bridge Leading Nowhere," *The San Diego Union-Tribune*, October 26, 1992.

John Carey, "There Just Aren't 'Enough Hearts to Go Around,'" *Business Week*, November 27, 1989.

Janice Castro, "Condition: Critical," *Time*, November 25, 1991.

Philip Elmer-Dewitt, "Oregon's Bitter Medicine," *Time*, August 17, 1992.

Mary Ann Elston, "Victorian Values and Animal Rights," *New Scientist*, May 23, 1992.

Roger W. Evans, Carlyn E. Orians, and Nancy L. Ascher,

"The Potential Supply of Organ Donors," *Journal of the American Medical Association*, January 8, 1992.

Barbara Fitzsimmons, "Did Baby Theresa Die in Vain?" *The San Diego Union-Tribune*, April 2, 1992.

Norman Fost and Ronald E. Cranford, "Hospital Ethics Committees," *Journal of the American Medical Association*, May 10, 1985.

Lawrence Galton, "The Amazing Story Behind the Medical Miracle of the Year: Heart Transplants," *Popular Science*, April 1968.

Judicial Council, "Guidelines for Ethics Committees in Health Care Institutions," *Journal of the American Medical Association*, May 10, 1985.

Prerna Mona Khanna, "Scarcity of Organs for Transplant Sparks a Move to Legalize Financial Incentives," *The Wall Street Journal*, September 8, 1992.

Charles Krauthammer, "Baby Theresa Stands Firm on a Frontier," *Los Angeles Times*, April 6, 1992.

Ron LaLonde, "Humans Could Get More Animal Organs," *Los Angeles Times*, July 9, 1992.

Pete Liepke, "Interview: Thomas Starzl," *Omni*, September 1990.

George D. Lundberg and Laurence Bodine, Esq., "Fifty Hours for the Poor," *Journal of the American Medical Association*, December 4, 1987.

Elliot Marshall, "Artificial Heart: The Beat Goes On," *Science*, August 2, 1991.

Lance Morrow, "When One Body Can Save Another," *Time*, June 17, 1991.

Edmund D. Pellegrino, "Medical Ethics," *Journal of the American Medical Association*, October 17, 1986.

Thomas G. Peters, "Life or Death: The Issue of Payment in Cadaveric Organ Donation," *Journal of the American*

Medical Association, March 13, 1991.

Fred Rosner, "Hospital Medical Ethics Committees: A Review of Their Development," *Journal of the American Medical Association*, May 10, 1985.

Marty Russo, "How to End the Health Care Crisis," *USA Today*, March 1992.

Joseph P. Shapiro, "To Ration or Not to Ration," *U.S. News & World Report*, August 10, 1992.

Aaron Spital, "The Shortage of Organs for Transplantation," *New England Journal of Medicine*, October 24, 1991.

Joel L. Swerdlow and Fred H. Cate, "Why Transplants Don't Happen," *The Atlantic*, October 1990.

UNOS Update, March-July 1992.

Robert M. Veatch, Ph.D., "Routine Inquiry About Organ Donation: An Alternative to Presumed Consent," *New England Journal of Medicine*, October 24, 1991.

Index

About the Author

Deanne Durrett is the author of the mid-grade novel *My New Sister the Bully*, stories and articles in magazines for adults as well as children, and newspaper feature stories, commentary, and columns. She has served as the Regional Advisor for the Society of Children's Book Writers in San Diego for more than three years.

Picture Credits